Hands, Wrists, Fingers

Hands, Wrists, Fingers

Creative Health for Musicians

Pedro de Alcantara

Anthem Press
An imprint of Wimbledon Publishing Company
www.anthempress.com

This edition first published in UK and USA 2026
by ANTHEM PRESS
75–76 Blackfriars Road, London SE1 8HA, UK
or PO Box 9779, London SW19 7ZG, UK
and
244 Madison Ave #116, New York, NY 10016, USA

© 2026 Pedro de Alcantara

The author asserts the moral right to be identified as the author of this work.

All rights reserved. Without limiting the rights under copyright reserved above, no part of this publication may be reproduced, stored or introduced into a retrieval system, or transmitted, in any form or by any means (electronic, mechanical, photocopying, recording or otherwise), without the prior written permission of both the copyright owner and the above publisher of this book.

British Library Cataloguing-in-Publication Data
A catalogue record for this book is available from the British Library.

Library of Congress Cataloging-in-Publication Data: 2025938140
A catalog record for this book has been requested.

ISBN-13: 978-1-83999-405-0 (Hbk)/ 978-1-83999-406-7(Pbk)
ISBN-10: 1-83999-405-3 (Hbk)/ 1-83999-406-1(Pbk)

Cover Credit: Hannes Eibinger from Pixabay

This title is also available as an eBook.

CONTENTS

Figures	vii
Acknowledgments	xv
Introduction: What Is Creative Health?	1

Part I: Culture — 9

1. A Paradigmatic Shift — 11
2. The Body Is Culture — 21
3. Discovery and Rediscovery — 39
4. The Power of Story — 53

Part II: The Language of the Hands — 69

5. Expressive Gesticulation — 71
6. Sounds Made and Sounds Heard — 87
7. The Dance — 97

Part III: Sensitivity and Creativity — 105

8. Textures — 107
9. Object Wisdom: A Manifesto — 119
10. Object Wisdom: A Workshop — 135
11. Strength Redefined — 149
12. Repetitive Practice — 165

Part IV: Knowledge and Mystery — 183

13. Energy — 185
14. Animality and Healing — 205

15. Ritual ... 221
16. Knowledge and Mystery ... 231
Conclusion ... 243
Appendix I: Illustrative Video Clips ... 249
Appendix II: Suggested Reading ... 253
Index ... 255

FIGURES

0.1	Flower child. Credit: Hai Nguyen	2
0.2	Playful children. Credit: Sasin Tinchai	3
0.3	Hand, spiral, circle. Credit: Willfried Wende	6
0.4	Creativity and commitment. Credit: Pexels	7
I	Happy child. Credit: Dmom	9
1.1	Intentionality and play. Credit: Pexels	12
1.2	Love and touch. Credit: Stocksnap	14
1.3	Handling life. Credit: Aamir Mohd Khan	16
1.4	Sensitive hands. Credit: Anonymous via Pixabay	17
1.5	Hands of connection. Credit: Use at your ease	19
2.1	The art of anatomy. Credit: commons.wikimedia.org	23
2.2	The art of acupunture. Credit: Matthias Frank	24
2.3	The art of chakras. Credit: Gerd Altmann	25
2.4	The art of tattoos. Anonymous via Pixabay	26
2.5	Reaching for the sun. Credit: John Hain	27
2.6	Skills of manicure. Credit: Frauke Riether	28
2.7	Touch of friendship. Credit: Dean Moriarty	30
2.8	Touch of communication. Credit: Alicja	30
2.9	Hands of elegance. Credit: Karolina Grabowska	32
2.10	Hands of ritual. Credit: Gaurav Kumar	33
2.11	The power of watches. Credit: Pexels	34

2.12	Tatooed upper limb. Credit: Photorama	36
2.13	Heart of henna. Credit: u_twa0qr4415	37
2.14	Henna and bangles. Credit: Irshad Rahimbux	37
2.15	Hands as palimpsest. Credit: Lisa Runnels	37
3.1	Enchantment of birth. Credit: Pexels	40
3.2	Enchantment of discovery. Credit: Julia Sezemova	41
3.3	Enchantment of connection. Credit: Anonymous via Pixabay	43
3.4	Enchantment of care. Credit: Pexels	44
3.5	Power of knuckles. Credit: Steward Masweneng	46
3.6	Power of claws. Credit: Artur Pawlak	48
3.7	Beauty of claws. Credit: Rethinktwice	48
3.8	Claws in context. Credit: G.C.	49
3.9	Extravagant claws. Credit: G.C.	49
3.10	Wonderment. Credit: Sally Wynn	51
3.11	Hands of commitment. Credit: Svklimkin	52
4.1	Cleansing hands. Credit: Henryk Niestrój	54
4.2	Raising a hand. Credit: Indus International School, Bangalore	55
4.3	Reaching for the light. Credit: Anonymous via Pixabay	56
4.4	From fear to love. Credit: ©Pedro de Alcantara	58
4.5	Left-handed daemon. Credit: Andreas	59
4.6	Hand aflame. Credit: Anonymous via Pixabay	61
4.7	Hands of craft. Credit: Enric Sagarra	62
4.8	Looming hands. Credit: Nowaja	63
4.9	Hands of sport. Credit: Pexels	63
4.10	The archer. Credit: Kathe Busk	64
4.11	Hands of clay. Credit: Pexels	65
4.12	Hands of closeness. Credit: Rijksmuseum	67

FIGURES

II	Speaking hands. Credit: Chu Viết Đôn	69
5.1	Hands of gesticulation. Credit: Rijksmuseum	72
5.2	Expressing joy. Credit: Rona Abdullah	73
5.3	Hands of dialogue. Credit: Magdalena Maier	76
5.4	Hands of conversation. Credit: Mircea Iancu	76
5.5	Hands of deep thought. Credit: Minh Huỳnh	78
5.6	Hands of dance. Credit: Shutterstock | Dmitry Rukhlenko	79
5.7	Commedia dell'arte. Credit: Brita Seifert	82
5.8	Hands of explanation. Credit: Wikimediaimage	83
5.9	Hands of peace. Credit: senjakelabu29	85
6.1	Youthful clapping. Credit: Dhanelle	89
6.2	Serious clapping. Credit: Yasdo	89
6.3	Sports clapping. Credit: Anonymous via Pixabay	89
6.4	Clapping of encouragement. Credit: stefanopanizzo	89
6.5	Traditional clapping. Credit: Jacqueline Macou	90
6.6	Crowd clapping. Credit: Gigxels	91
6.7	Big ears. Credit: Holger Kraft	93
6.8	Megaphone hands. Credit: Luisella Planeta LOVE PEACE	94
6.9	Megaphone man. Credit: Harald Funken	94
6.10	Noisy bird. Credit: ivabalk	94
6.11	Hands of aural protection. Credit: Shutterstock | Studio Grand Web	94
6.12	Silliness. Credit: Michael Kopp	95
7.1	Walking finger. Credit: Shutterstock | Montira Areepongthum	99
7.2	Dancers. Credit: Evgen Rom	99
7.3	Flexed wrists. Credit: Myriams-fotos	101
7.4	Arms and flexed wrists. Credit: Ronald Plett	101

7.5	Intertwining. Credit: Pexels	101
7.6	Flexed wrist and texture. Credit: Mabel Amber	101
7.7	Flamenco. Credit: Iatya Prunkova	103
7.8	Octopus. Credit: Erik Tanghe	103
III	Capable hands. Credit: Keith Johnston	105
8.1	Peeling hands. Credit: congerdesign	108
8.2	Texture of fibres. Credit: wal_172619	110
8.3	Texture of textile. Credit: Gundula Vogel	110
8.4	Texture of fabric. Credit: hartono subagio	111
8.5	Hand sensing layers. Credit: Rijksmuseum	112
8.6	Hand sensing an instrument. Credit: Rijksmuseum	113
8.7	Papers. Credit: Sergii Koviarov	114
8.8	Object textures. Credit: ©Pedro de Alcantara	116
8.9	Hands and fine sand. Credit: Gisela Merkuur	117
8.10	Hands on strings. Credit: Franz P. Sauerteig	118
9.1	Pruning shears. Credit: K47	120
9.2	Calligraphy brush. Credit: Thierry Raimbault	121
9.3	Fabric and button. Credit: yaoyaoyao5yaoyaoyao	123
9.4	Drawknife. Credit: Graham Hobster	125
9.5	Hands of music. Credit: Bea Hutchins	126
9.6	Tree of flutes. Credit: Arjun Jaisawal	127
9.7	Pan flute. Credit: Stocksnap	128
9.8	Silver flute. Credit: José Arroyo	128
9.9	Old Joe. Credit: Peter H	130
9.10	Wisdom of naiveté. Credit: thedanw	132
9.11	Object wisdom and poise. Credit: ymyphoto	133
10.1	Juggling balls. Credit: ©Pedro de Alcantara	136

FIGURES

10.2	Tennis ball. Credit: Stocksnap	138
10.3	Baseball. Credit: Francisco Corado Rivera	138
10.4	Cherished objects. Credit: ©Pedro de Alcantara	140
10.5	Page flipping. Credit: Petra	142
10.6	Thread. Credit: congerdesign	143
10.7	Young flutist. Credit: Rijksmuseum	146
10.8	Handle. Credit: Ornella Sannazzaro	147
10.9	Guitar. Credit: bustaluiggi	147
10.10	Pen. Credit: Rijksmuseum	147
10.11	Wind instrument. Credit: Jacqueline Macou	147
11.1	Geodesic dome. Credit: Eduardo Ponce De Leon	150
11.2	Tensegrity sculpture. Credit: commons.wikimedia.org	150
11.3	Distributed resistance. Credit: Nur Aziz Arifin	152
11.4	Resistance and poise. Credit: Artsy Solomon	152
11.5	Resistance, poise, and love. Credit: Tamotoji	152
11.6	Resistance and communication. Credit: Chris Thornton	152
11.7	Whole-body power. Credit: Anonymous via Pixabay	154
11.8	Distributed effort. Credit: Hiep Hong	154
11.9	Whole-body poise. Credit: Jupi Lu	155
11.10	Rubber bands. Credit: Stocksnap	156
11.11	Newspaper. Credit: Victoria	158
11.12	Crumpled. Credit: Anonymous via Pixabay	160
11.13	Kneading. Credit: Anonymous via Pixabay	162
12.1	A grid of choices. Credit: χρίς	167
12.2	Varied gradations. Credit: Marijana	169
12.3	Organized gradations. Credit: Franck Barske	169
12.4	Relaxed focus. Credit: Jiradet Inrungruan	171

12.5	Monkey mind. Credit: sharkolot	174
12.6	Beans, one by one. Credit: Daniel Ramirez	176
12.7	A collection of beans. Credit: Gideon Putra	177
12.8	Varied beans. Credit: Pexels	178
12.9	Collected beans. Credit: sandrinessouza	179
12.10	Reliable repetition. Credit: Pete Linforth	181
12.11	Built-in repetition. Credit: Taken	181
IV	Connection. Credit: Olcay Ertem	183
13.1	Energy of touch. Credit: Heung Soon	186
13.2	Energy of pointing. Credit: Rapheal Nathaniel	188
13.3	Speaking and pointing. Credit: Rob Slaven	188
13.4	Focused pointing. Credit: Mojca-peter	190
13.5	Distance pointing. Credit: Mojca-peter	191
13.6	Hands of heat. Credit: Gerd Altmann	192
13.7	Hnads of cold. Credit: Roland Mey	193
13.8	Light. Credit: GRELOT71	194
13.9	Heavy. Credit: Felix Mittermeier	195
13.10	Propagation. Credit: ©Pedro de Alcantara	196
13.11	Containment. Credit: Meredin	196
13.12	Appearing. Credit: Adil Abib	198
13.13	Disappearing. Credit: Sergio Cerrato	199
13.14	Fighting. Credit: Herbert Aust	201
13.15	Dancing. Credit: Pexels	202
13.16	Collected possibilities. Credit: Bernd Hildebrandt	204
14.1	Owl in flight. Credit: Danny Moore	206
14.2	Purr and growl. Credit: Thomas Wolter	206
14.3	Intuitive play. Credit: Anonymous via Pixabay	207

14.4	Cat girl. Credit: Anonymous via Pixabay	208
14.5	Cat being cuddled. Credit: Fuzzy Rescue	209
14.6	Paw and hand. Credit: giselastillhard	210
14.7	Animal and child. Credit: Lenka Novotná	210
14.8	Child and teddy. Credit: Petra	211
14.9	Enveloped baby. Credit: Adele Morris	213
14.10	Enveloped flowers. Credit: Thinh Nguyen Gia	214
14.11	Enveloped chest. Credit: Aathif Aarifeen	215
14.12	Enveloped love. Credit: Ian Lindsay	217
14.13	Animal hand. Credit: Torgeir	218
14.14	Splashing animal. Credit: Roman Kogomachenko	219
14.15	Lighted hand. Credit: Michael Treu	219
15.1	Coffee cup. Credit: Anja	222
15.2	In the river. Credit: Sasin Tipchai	223
15.3	Child drawing. Credit: Thomas G.	225
15.4	Cellist. Credit: Ri Butov	226
15.5	Brushing a horse. Credit: Alexa	227
15.6	Blowing bubbles. Credit: Daniela Dimitrova	229
15.7	Ritualized life. Credit: Ri Butov	229
16.1	Liminality. Credit: Luca Finardi	232
16.2	A liminal entity. Credit: fr.m.wikipedia.org	233
16.3	A liminal passage. Credit: Ariel Hii	234
16.4	Stepping into the void. Credit: Melissa G	237
16.5	Lined palm. Credit: wal_172619	238
16.6	The Guidonian hand. Credit: en.wikipedia.org	239
16.7	Knowledge and mystery at work. Credit: Vinit Kumar	241
C.1	Marvel. Credit: Swastik Arora	244

C.2	Unified purpose. Credit: sarab123	244
C.3	The growth of unified purpose. Credit: Ben Kerckx	244
C.4	The results of imagination. Credit: Christopher Chilton	245
C.5	Infinite potentiality. Credit: Rosalia Ricotta	246

ACKNOWLEDGMENTS

Hands, Wrists, Fingers is the result of decades of exploration, learning, and sharing. Many students and colleagues tested these materials and contributed to their development. I think of this book as "our project," a vast collaborative effort.

The book is illustrated with a plethora of photos. Most of them are sourced from Pixabay.com, a site where skillful photographers share their beautiful images for free and without copyright restrictions. I'm grateful to these generous photographers, although they might never know how much their work has helped me.

The team at Anthem Press offered me clarity and support. I'd like to thank Jebaslin Hephzibah, Golda Merline, Mario Rosair, and Tej P. S. Sood.

My wife Alexis Niki is my trusty soundboard and companion. Our hands are forever intertwined.

Pedro de Alcantara
Paris, May 31, 2025.

INTRODUCTION

What Is Creative Health?

Are you in pain? Creative Health may be able to help. But first, let me speak more generally.

Creative Health is a way of paying attention. Creative Health is *what* you do, *how* you do it, and *who you are* as you do it. This means that Creative Health is all-encompassing: your dynamic response to everything that happens in your day and everything that happens in your musical life.

For some people, health might mean a series of numbers: red blood cell counts, cholesterol, weight, blood pressure. If your numbers are okay, you're okay. This is a narrow definition, and I'm using it here just to make an argument. It doesn't matter if few people believe in this definition.

For other people, health is a broader concept. Diet and exercise, relationships, sleep patterns; posture, manner of dress, manner of speech; family life, work life, spiritual life: the list is long. You might have an unhealthy job, for instance, or be in an unhealthy relationship; your bed might be uncomfortable and causing you short-term or long-term harm; you might be addicted to irritation and frustration, to cynicism and arrogance. Health, good and bad, becomes synonymous with your entire existence. And taking care of your broadly defined health is a full-time job.

It's possible to have a healthy or unhealthy relationship with your musical instrument, with your colleagues, with the stage; with the scores that you study and interpret; with the totality of your career. You might hate Beethoven, for instance—and you wouldn't be the only person on Earth to hate him. And if your symphony orchestra programs his symphonies year after year after year, you might also grow to hate your job and your life. Beethoven is one example among many. Every composer, every composition, every sound, and every gesture is forever making you healthier or unhealthier.

One day a new conductor takes over, a couple of the ornery woodwind players are replaced with fine talented musicians, the theater provides comfortable chairs for the orchestra players, and on your own, you find a way of lessening or eliminating your asthma. You might fall in love with Beethoven and discover his symphonies as if for the first time. "Beethoven, wow!" Creative Health invites change and allows it.

Many classically trained musicians tend to play exclusively from scores: no playing by ear, no improvising, no arranging, no transposing; nothing but the score. And many of these musicians have a horror of the very idea of improvising. "No, not me, *never*!" Healthy or unhealthy? Other musicians, comfortable with improvisation and playing by ear, have a horror of theory, analysis, and the technical vocabulary of music. "Don't talk to me about solfège. Oh, how I hate it!" Healthy or unhealthy?

Let's abbreviate the principle: "Health is everything" (Figure 0.1).

Creativity, too, can be defined broadly or narrowly. I subscribe to a broad definition. A newborn is an extremely creative individual, making thousands of neural connections minute by minute and creating an entire world from scratch. The newborn is a demiurge—that is, an intermediary between the invisible laws of nature and the visible, material world. From a tremendous number of difficult-to-interpret bits of information, the newborn perceives the world and gives it order and meaning. You only need to look at a newborn's face to see the creative mind at work.

People are forever creating businesses, philosophies, recipes, sandcastles, objects, tools, neologisms, interpretations, procedures, problems, and solutions. To speak, for instance, is to be creative; among other things, you create sounds out of silent thoughts, and you create infinitely varied phrases and

Figure 0.1 Flower child. Credit: Hai Nguyen.

sentences as you communicate your thoughts and feelings. It's by no means banal. Since we're talking about communication, to gossip is to be creative—which shows that not everything ever created is praiseworthy. Enmity, fear, hatred, and complete chaos are all products of creative minds. Creators might make judgments, and fellow human beings might pass judgments on the results of creativity. But creativity itself is free from judgment. It doesn't necessarily create good things; it creates.

Let's abbreviate the principle: "Creativity is everything."

Creative Health is a sort of interaction between two forces that exist beyond the confines of time and space. Creativity and health both existed before your birth, and they will both survive your passing away. Interestingly, their interaction is immediate and local: right here, right now, what are you doing? How are you feeling? What are your perceptions of the situation in which you find yourself? What decisions are you going to make regarding Beethoven and anything else that you're dealing with? How are you going to implement those decisions in practice? This is Creative Health: your response to the moment, and to the accumulation of unbroken moments that is synonymous with your life.

Let's abbreviate the principle: "Creative Health is everything" (Figure 0.2).

Any decision that you make affects your health positively or negatively. The effect may be huge (you decide to quit your job) or tiny (you decide to take a breath), but there'll be an effect either way. Making decisions isn't

Figure 0.2 Playful children. Credit: Sasin Tinchai.

always a matter of the conscious mind. We'll see in Chapter 14 how your inner animal makes a great many decisions that your intellect might not even notice. A decision of yours might brew slowly for a long time, until it crystallizes into action. A historian once said that the decline of the Roman Empire happened gradually and suddenly. Creative Health is just like that: gradual and sudden. A shout seems sudden, but it might have taken you 30 years to gather its power. Is it healthy for you to shout? It depends. Is it healthy for you not to shout? It depends. But we might say that your Creative Health does need to have a great many things in reserve, ready to come out even if you never deploy them.

The healthy individual has latencies: a big vocabulary, a big toolbox, a deep well of energies, talents, memories, and stories, a big database of gestures and postures. Could you live productively and comfortably if your hands were only able to perform six or eight distinct gestures? Let's pick a large number, like 144,000. If you have these many gestures at your disposal, you can do pretty much anything and everything, even if in your daily life you only use 1 percent (about 1,400 gestures, say) of the possibilities inside you. Creative Health is a big database readily available to you. *Hands, Wrists, Fingers* will help you develop your databases of linguistically animated gestures (Chapters 5, 6, and 7), of energies (Chapter 13), of strategies for practicing (Chapter 12).

Your hands, wrists, and fingers are central to your Creative Health, musical or otherwise. Your mind and heart have wishes; your hands, wrists, and fingers express your wishes and fulfill them. Hands are so important and so wondrous that they merit veneration. But the hands are literally indivisible from the totality of yourself; they do not exist and cannot exist separately from the rest of you. Your fingers are always obeying your mind and your heart. Even when they seem to disobey you, they're still responding to something in you: doubt, confusion, incoherence, fear, anger, ambiguity, and many other energies. Creative Health requires a constant effort toward clarity and coherence, both of which you can enhance by becoming alert to the stories that you tell about the world and about your own self (Chapters 2, 3, and 4).

Coherent mind and heart, coherent hands, wrists, and fingers. It's why we venerate great musicians: because they've achieved coherence. It's misleading to look closely at the incredible hands of concert pianists and try to imitate exactly what their hands are doing. You won't be able to have their fingers if you don't have their hearts. And the only heart you'll ever have is your own. Creative Health is a pursuit of the first person, singular: "I have a heart. And I have hands, wrists, and fingers. I play, I make sounds, I connect with music and with the audience." The mysteries of creative connection are many. *Hands, Wrists, Fingers* will help you confront and embody these mysteries (Chapters 15 and 16).

Creative Health is a deeply psychological pursuit. There's a music score in front of your eyes. What do you see? What do you say to yourself when you see what you see? What happens to your brain, your heart, your fingertips when you're faced with the score? Wonderment and puzzlement; enlightenment and confusion; appreciation and indifference; joy and despair; love and hate. Hands, wrists, and fingers are intertwined with every emotion that the score elicits in you. Sight-reading elicits emotions. Playing the same old piece again and again elicits emotions. Creative Health might one day require that you throw a score in the garbage—which for many musicians is almost impossible to do. Let's stretch the principle a little too far: "Your reactions about music itself can give you tendonitis." Creative Health is your capacity to recognize this eventuality and work through its difficulties; to recognize dozens or hundreds of eventualities and work through their difficulties and their integrative potentialities (Chapter 1).

Suppose that I ask you to improvise an eight-bar phrase in the style of Mozart, in E-flat major but with a brief visit to C minor, using triple time in Andante Moderato, like a love aria in an opera: the soprano is in love (E-flat major), the tenor isn't paying attention to her (C minor), but—you know, hope shall prevail (E-flat major). I've created a situation; you started reacting to it the moment I said the word "improvise," and your hands, wrists, and fingers started looking for the exit door. Creative Health acknowledges your first reaction and respects it. Creative Health then allows you to identify some of the choices at your disposal: "Forget about it!" "Wait, tell me again, slowly, please." "Give me the start of the phrase, I'll finish it." "Nah, you do it." "Can we change the subject?" "Here's my attempt. Who knows what'll come out!" Creative Health doesn't judge you if you have a meltdown or if you play the most un-Mozartian phrase in the history of music. Creative Health is all-forgiving and all-embracing. And Creative Health might also help you learn how to improvise if you wish.

I don't mean that you *should* improvise, or that you *should not* improvise. I mean that your life is situational, and your reactions to the thousand situations are central to your well-being. Creative Health to the rescue! (Figure 0.3)

I'm ready to tell you more about hands, wrists, and fingers that are hurting and what you can expect from reading this book as regards healing.

A writer famously said that all happy families are alike; each unhappy family is unhappy in its own way (*Anna Karenina*, Tolstoy). I'd like to adapt the saying: All healthy hands are alike; each hurting hand is hurting in its own way. When it comes to your hands, your talents and travails are uniquely yours, and your path forward away from pain will be uniquely yours, too. You're likely to need your own combination of therapies and procedures. My book provides a database of observations and exercises that are potentially useful to all readers, although each reader will make a singular use of the total database.

Figure 0.3 Hand, spiral, circle. Credit: Willfried Wende.

You'll learn about developing more sensitive hands, in part through the development of gradations: knowing how to do nothing, knowing how to do just a little bit, knowing how to do as much as needed.

You'll learn how to develop interesting and pleasant relationships with the objects in your life, including those musical instruments that your hands sometimes consider the source of pain. Among other things, you'll play with juggling balls, not to juggle but to learn the art of rotations, twists, and turns—which I consider essential for daily life and for playing any musical instrument.

You'll redefine strength, away from the notion of muscle power and toward the notion of distributed resistance and mobility.

You'll learn how to provide your hands with comforting reassurance, a sort of healing energy that comes from the timeless pleasures of enveloping and being enveloped.

You'll learn to trust your inner animal, an intelligent entity residing deeply inside you. The inner animal has remarkable innate talents for healing itself and offering healing to others.

You'll learn to create a little distance between you and the pain in your hands, partly by practicing the art of telling stories about your hands. Distance helps dissipation by making things smaller. It's said that time heals all wounds. This strikes me as neither practical nor realistic. But distance does lessen many wounds, even if only temporarily.

You'll learn how to infuse your gestures with greater linguistic clarity. Hands hurt less when they know *how* to say *what* they're trying to say.

You'll learn how to tap into your talent for humor, discovery, and ingenuity. You might invent new ways of playing and of healing your aches and pains, including ways that I have never imagined. It all starts with a paradigm shift, which is a change of mind and a change of heart (Figure 0.4).

Figure 0.4 Creativity and commitment. Credit: Pexels.

Part I
CULTURE

Figure I Happy child. Credit: DMom.

Chapter 1

A PARADIGMATIC SHIFT

A paradigm may be informally defined as a set of values, concepts, and priorities. The set of values determines your perspective in life and your practical behaviors; you do as you believe. Different musicians think and play differently because they apply different values, concepts, and priorities to their music making. Glenn Gould and Artur Rubinstein lived according to different paradigms. We might not completely understand all the intricacies of their respective paradigms, but we know that they were different from the other. We can see and hear the differences, and we can tell them apart from a single note or a single phrase of music played by each of them. In addition to their music making, their entire existences were lived according to their individual paradigms.

We might liken your paradigm to a master puppeteer, in command of your actions. Your aspirations and motivations, your habits and routines, your choices and decisions, your repertory, your career, your practicing and performing, your sounds, your rubato, your articulations and dynamics: all of it is determined by your paradigm. But you're not the unwilling victim of the puppeteer, because you're the puppeteer yourself. It's possible—and I'd say urgently necessary—for you to become alert to your paradigm, and for you to play with it, so to speak (Figure 1.1).

Simplifying greatly and perhaps dangerously, I'd like to contrast two foundational paradigms for musicians. The first one is physical and mechanical: the health of your hands, wrists, and fingers is a matter of a well-maintained body that is alert to movement, reflex, physical relaxation, and other dimensions of coordination. This paradigm comes with exercises, attitudes, habits, ways of working, and disciplines. It includes finger and wrist exercises, stretches, and a warm-up routine. Its theoretical underpinning comes from anatomy and physiology. And its mood, its tone of voice, its general attitude might be called *left brain*: facts and materials, metrics, technicalities.

I'll quote an imaginary left-brained musician of a certain type.

Figure 1.1 Intentionality and play. Credit: Pexels.

My left index finger is inflamed, and my wrist is tight. I'll start my day by soaking my hands and arms in warm water, followed by ten minutes of stretches. Then I'll practice slow steady scales in major and minor keys, aiming for absolute evenness of sound and technical reliability. Every day a different key: today, C major and A minor; tomorrow, F major and D minor. After 25 minutes of practice, a five-minute break. After two blocks of practice time, I'll again soak my hands and arms in warm water. Three hours of practice in the morning, two in the afternoon if I don't have rehearsals, in which case I'll do the two extra hours after dinner.

The second paradigm is holistic: your health comes from a creative response to a creative situation or stimulus, which may be a phrase, a composition, an improvisation, a musical style, a musical challenge, the situation of the concert stage, your relationship with the audience, and your relationship with music itself. This paradigm also comes with exercises, perceptions, and ways of practicing and performing. The holistic paradigm has so many interlocking dimensions that it doesn't lend itself to abbreviated descriptions. But let's call it a *right-brain* attitude, in which the materiality of facts is secondary to wonderment, mystery, imaginings, memories, and stories.

A PARADIGMATIC SHIFT

Now I'll quote an imaginary right-brained musician of a certain type. Honestly, this is me, talking about myself.

My fingers and I go back a long way. I still remember when my right hand was too elastic, too supple for me to hold the cello bow comfortably. The *boneless chicken in flight*, I called it. Recently I've been playing these wonderful and bizarre compositions that are somehow changing the shape of my right hand. It's freaky, though it feels great. The boneless chicken is receiving a highly functional skeleton that seems to respond immediately to the least stimulation from my brain. Chicken cyborg—that's me, through and through. No, I can't explain it any better. This happens to be the best explanation for how I'm working and how I'm feeling.

In this strange paradigm, hands aren't primarily a physical instrument but a creative instrument. They speak and sing with their own intelligence, reacting to the originative stimulations of life and music. Hands have personalities, complete with quirks, likes and dislikes, friends and enemies.

When it comes to exercising your hands within this paradigm, instead of stretching your fingers you say with your hands something that requires, for the full expression of its meaning, a stretch between fingers: "Live Long and Prosper." This is the Vulcan greeting, popularized by Leonard Nimoy's character Mr. Spock in the original *Star Trek* TV show. Index and middle fingers close together, ring and little fingers close together, a big space between middle and ring fingers, a big space between thumb and index, the hand raised with the open palm facing outward. Nimoy developed the gesture himself, inspired by dimensions of the Jewish religious life he grew up with. The gesture, then, is infused with psychological and metaphysical energies, with an undeniable element of narrative and storytelling. The gesture is primarily *linguistic*, and the positioning of fingers and the motor organization of the gesture is a response to something meaningful that you wish to say. All the same, the gesture does require a motor organization, a physicality, and a technique. It's very interesting to note that some people find it quite difficult to re-create the gesture and gather the fingers in their required positions. The fingers seem to disobey the brain, as it were: they don't want to come together or to separate; they become wobbly or jagged, and the final gesture is stiff and awkward. It takes practice to perform the gesture comfortably.

As it happens, Mr. Spock's gesture is positive and life-affirming. But gestures meant to provoke and insult also come with their own motor organization, their stretches and challenges. The idea is to infuse all your gestures

Figure 1.2 Love and touch. Credit: StockSnap.

with a linguistic energy, positive or negative as it may be—*all* your gestures, including a single note played on the piano or the trumpet (Figure 1.2).

This linguistic organization of gesture is ever-present: in the way we greet people, in handshakes, in insults that we give with various finger combinations; in flamenco and the classical dances of India, Cambodia, and a hundred other cultures; with umpires and referees, indicating a foul or an offside, for instance; and in endless situations in every culture. It's completely normal for us to use our arms, hands, wrists, and fingers linguistically. And yet, sometimes we forget or neglect this linguistic dimension, focusing too much on the physical sensations of gesture and—when things go wrong—with the pains and aches of gestures. These pains and aches, which sometimes are truly debilitating, give us the feeling—no, the *certainty*—that we have a physical problem. And since this clearly is the case (we feel *absolutely certain* of it), then we need a physical solution to this grave problem of ours.

I posit that the restoration of linguistic energies to gesture is a possible remedy to the pains and aches of gestures gone wrong. Let me go too far with my claims and say half-flippantly and half-seriously that you suffer tendonitis (or other conditions of this type) when your gestures have lost their linguistic, psychological, sociocultural, and metaphysical dimensions. The tendonitis is a call toward the integrative regeneration of the whole person.

In a holistic paradigm, pains and aches aren't physical. Instead, they're the apparently physical manifestations of an existential problem or situation. I say "apparently" because the disjunction between body and mind is a sort of illusion. Nothing is ever physical, nothing is ever mental, nothing is ever spiritual: everything is always intertwined.

You might feel that the tendonitis, the frozen shoulder, and the herniated disk are primarily physical, or at least physical in origin. But the herniated disk happened to coincide with your looming retirement, or the looming adoption of a baby from a foreign land, or the looming audition or competition, or the looming deadline to submit a composition to a publisher.

And the tendonitis somehow reflects a desire to play fast and loud, faster and louder than other people, as fast and as loud as another musician whom you admire a little, envy a tad, and hate a lot, although you can't bring yourself to admit honestly that you feel hatred in your heart. Your tendonitis might be the reflection of aesthetic choices, a taste for certain sounds and interpretations, the feeling or the conviction that to express yourself you really, *really* need to dig into that instrument and make those sounds come out whether they want to come out or not.

Your frozen shoulder might be telling you that you feel ambivalent about your work schedule, about the tours and the group dynamics in the orchestra, about the conductor, or even about music itself, because if you think about it, you never wanted to become a professional musician to begin with. It was what your father wanted for you, but somehow you didn't have the means back then to say "NO!" to your father and to pursue your own interests instead. Rightly or wrongly, I'm going to insist that there's no separation between the body, the mind, and the soul; between your way of doing things and the narrative behind your way of doing things; between your way of doing things and all your sensations and feelings, including pain and joy (Figure 1.3).

Integrative exercises for the hands, wrists, and fingers require their own physicality. The exercises involve jokes and stories, games, explorations, meditations, situations, provocations, and invitations. Their ultimate purpose is not to provide you with physical relaxation, but with psychophysical, creative, and existential fulfillment.

Will these concepts and exercises work for you? There are no guarantees. People really are different in the way they think, feel, react, and move. To the old paradigm, the new paradigm is incomprehensible, absurd, and ridiculous. To deny that physical pain requires physical healing seems downright perverted. At the very least, though, you might want to "visit my paradigm while on holiday from yours." The quotation marks indicate that the expression is a

Figure 1.3 Handling life. Credit: Aamir Mohd Khan.

joke that's not a joke, and they also indicate that your holiday might presage a permanent move to the new paradigm.

There are risks and dangers in every situation, without exception. Suppose I offer you a glass of tap water. Perhaps there's some lead in the pipes, unbeknownst to the two of us. Perhaps you expect cool water, but the water is lukewarm. Do you know how horrible it is to drink something lukewarm when you expect and desire something cool? Or perhaps you take too large a mouthful of water. It hurts your throat, your whole vocal tract. Or perhaps you drink a bit too quickly and sloppily, spilling water on your shirt. Or perhaps you drop and break the glass on account of an inattentive or hurried gesture. All of us have broken glasses here and there in our lives; strictly speaking, every time we hold a glass there's some risk that we might drop it and break it.

The risks and dangers associated with accepting a glass of water are small and generally easy to navigate. You're willing to take them because you're thirsty and because you know that most likely you won't hurt yourself in the process. But the main thing is to acknowledge that these risks do exist.

Once you start thinking about it, you'll see that there are no situations, no actions, no thoughts, and no words that are completely free from all risk. It's simply not possible. To say "good morning" to a stranger is a risk; not to say "good morning" to a stranger is a different risk. To cross the street is a risk; to get out of the bathtub is a risk; to live in New York is a risk; to live in any other city in the whole world comes with its own risks. To practice the violin

Figure 1.4 Sensitive hands. Credit: Anonymous via Pixabay.

for four hours is a risk. To avoid practicing is a whole other risk, with different consequences and effects (Figure 1.4).

Logically, every paradigm carries risks and dangers. A materialistic musician could develop a brilliant instrumental technique that lacks soul and meaning. Ignoring sensations, sentiments, intuitions, insights, and the difficult-to-describe exigencies of the symbolic realm, materialists risk painting themselves into a corner. The search for technical brilliance has often turned musicians into dissatisfied perfectionists, highly judgmental of themselves and other people, never happy, never at ease, never fulfilled, and always suffering—even when they play very well. The great difficulty is that their suffering is caused by the paradigm they espouse, whether they're alert to it or not.

When it comes to confronting their suffering and overcoming it, musicians need to deal with "paradigm separation anxiety," to coin a term. The paradigm is causing you much suffering; you're the master puppeteer yourself, the entity in charge of the control and the entity being controlled; you can only stop suffering if you leave your habitual paradigm behind and become a different master puppeteer—that is, a different person. It's not easy.

Our holistic paradigm, sensorial and intuitive, carries its own risks and dangers. You might get lost in a subjective head trip triggered by a flood of emotions and stories. Then you'll forget your homework, the obligation to master the intricacies of your instrument and your voice, the practicalities of how you handle your flute or your cello. Intuitions and stories, sure, but how to embody them in practice? How to get out of your head and join the hustle and bustle?

I don't propose that you deny the existence of physicality or the merits of the analytical, organized left brain. I don't propose that you invest all your energies in the intuitions, sensations, and stories of the diffused right brain. I don't propose that you stop consulting with doctors, physical therapists, and hand specialists. I don't propose that you ignore the marvels of technique and dexterity, the nitty-gritty of instrumental mastery. My proposed paradigm is complex, requiring metaphors and similes, indirect approaches, evasions. With any luck, the paradigm will become clearer as we go through the book together. But here is an incomplete list of my proposals. I'll number them, partly to please the list-loving left brain that dwells in the mind of every reader.

1. I propose that constant alertness to the moment is a duty and a right, an obligation and a pleasure.
2. I propose that alertness is a game, delightful to play but sometimes difficult to grasp. Work is play, and play is work. What are the rules? It's not so simple.
3. I propose that every gesture—every single gesture!—may be animated by a linguistic impulse.
4. I propose that the linguistic impulse is embodied. It breathes, it moves, it takes on shapes. The linguistic impulse is dynamic and elastic, changeable, lively, animal.
5. I propose that every paradigm is based on an intricate web of arguments and narratives. For better and for worse, in *Hands, Wrists, Fingers* I go deep into the stories that shape my paradigm and give it coherence and strength.
6. I propose that gestures have specific dimensions, inseparable from their practical context; and general dimensions that don't depend on context. Flute fingers and cello fingers are totally different in some ways, and totally alike in other ways. In *Hands, Wrists, Fingers* I focus on the general dimensions of gesture, hardly mentioning the specificity of gestures in specialized contexts. Truth be told, I'll never mention specific gestures.
7. I propose that good health is a balance between improvisation and structure, broadly defined. The improvisation comes from the creator in you; the structure comes from the editor in you. They can work so well together that sometimes you won't be able to tell them apart.
8. I propose that alertness to the linguistic impulse is infused with curiosity, wonderment, and gratitude. Life is incredible; the way our hands, wrists, and fingers react to the musical language is incredible.

Figure 1.5 Hands of connection. Credit: Use at your ease.

9. I propose that creative health is full of paradoxes. You *must think* about your hands, wrists, and fingers, and you *must stop thinking* about your hands, wrists, and fingers.
10. I propose that creative health comes from your initiative or agency: your ability to make choices and decisions and to act on your own behalf note by note, gesture by gesture.

Let's see how we can integrate these proposals into a living, pulsating, practical paradigm (Figure 1.5).

Chapter 2

THE BODY IS CULTURE

In my student days, I met a sensitive Argentinian my age who told me something I'll never forget. He had grown up in a conservative religious household. From as far back as he could remember, he had been trained to walk close to the buildings out in the street, rather than in the middle of the sidewalk or near the curb; and to walk with his head down, his eyes on the ground. If he walked upright and in the middle of the sidewalk, head high and eyes alert to the world, God would think that the young man was occupying too much space and was being presumptuous and disrespectful, and he (the young man) should expect to be punished.

Within our distinct cultures, we're permanently engaged in a dynamic play of opposing forces, sometimes harmoniously, sometimes awkwardly. My wife is taller than average. Years ago, a creative learning situation led her to a sudden realization: "I have the right to occupy *all* of my space!" Until then, she had unconsciously strived to make herself smaller due to implicit family and societal pressures. There followed a demanding process of recalibration and regrowth, which was by no means pain-free. A friend of mine, also taller than average, once shared something similar and yet quite different. He told me that people often equated height with strength, which made it harder for family, friends, and strangers to recognize the emotional vulnerability that he carried within. As a result, he had long felt misunderstood and unseen. He admitted that, given a choice, he would prefer to be shorter.

Posture, movement, gesture, body language, clothes, makeup, sexuality, biological functioning, self-worth, health and illness: all human dimensions are deeply intertwined in a totality partly determined by family dynamics and social norms—or, to put it differently, by culture. There are cultural communities of self-effacement and communities of self-expression. Some cultures allow for extraversion. Others require it: introversion is against the culture and it might even be considered an illness. Some cultures say, "Be skinny, or else." Others say, "Health and prosperity equals big. Don't be skinny, or else!" Some cultures bring sexuality to the fore. Others suppress it, sometimes subtly, sometimes brutally. In some cultures, sitting straight is the mark of a good upbringing. In others, it's a sign of arrogance and hostility toward others, of standing apart, of displaying unwarranted high status. "We don't do that here."

In your exploration of Creative Health, you'll need to bring your innermost culture to the fore, the better to understand where you're coming from and where you're going.

The Round Table

Let's imagine a round table of experts, discussing the workings of the body—or, more precisely, its very nature. We'll invite a Western anatomist, an acupuncturist, a yogi, and a mystic. The anatomist will describe bones, ligaments, tendons, muscles, cartilage, fascia, and other components of the human body that most of us are generally or vaguely familiar with. The description will be illustrated with charts, drawings, perhaps a plastic model of a flayed body part showing details of its anatomy. The anatomist's vocabulary is vast and detailed: the femur, the tibia, the patella; the clavicle, the scapula, the coccyx (Figure 2.1).

The acupuncturist will talk about meridians, energies, the Qi or Chi, yin and yang, heaven and earth. It's interesting: the anatomist uses a lot of Latin words, while the acupuncturist uses a lot of Chinese words. It doesn't matter if the two of them are American or German or Brazilian: the vocabulary they employ is inseparable from the concepts that they espouse, reflecting the culture in which the concepts arose over decades, centuries, and millennia. For a certain view of life, you must rely on Latin words; for another view of life, you can't avoid Chinese words. To varying degrees, we all absorb these foreign discoveries, beliefs, and vocabularies. But the anatomist and the acupuncturist think and talk very differently one from the other, because the body of the anatomist isn't the body of the acupuncturist—I mean, their concept of the body, their concept of health, their concept of life (Figure 2.2).

In our imaginary round table, the yogi will speak after the anatomist and the acupuncturist. We'll imagine that he or she will tell us about the chakras: energy centers, the understanding of which originated in ancient Indian traditions. A widely disseminated version considers that there are seven main chakras, aligned along the spine from the base to the crown of the head and governing varied aspects of life. Balanced chakras are the cause and the manifestation of good health. Unbalanced and blocked chakras are the cause and the manifestation of ill health. Inevitably, the yogi will share with us a specific vocabulary, which will be foreign to many people in the audience. The words come from Sanskrit, a venerable language of beauty and power.

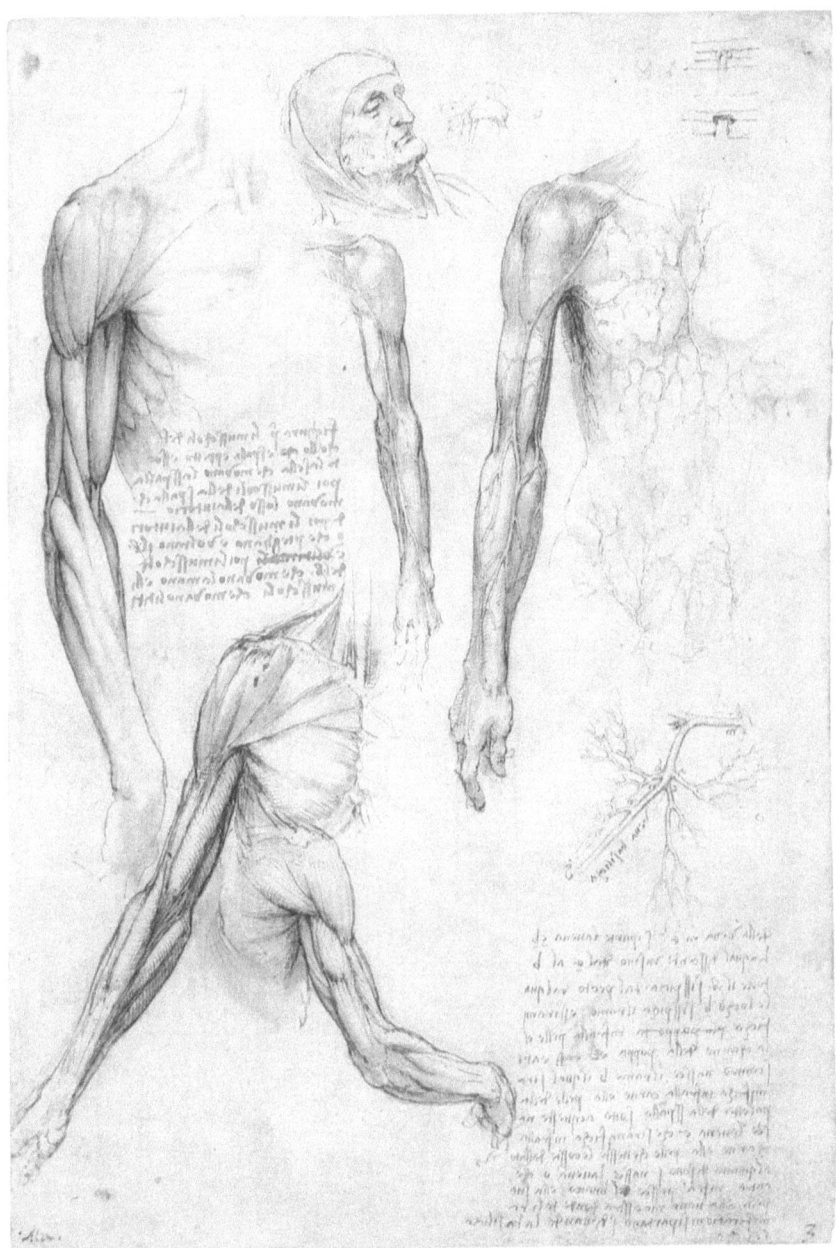

Figure 2.1 The art of anatomy. Credit: commons.wikimedia.org.

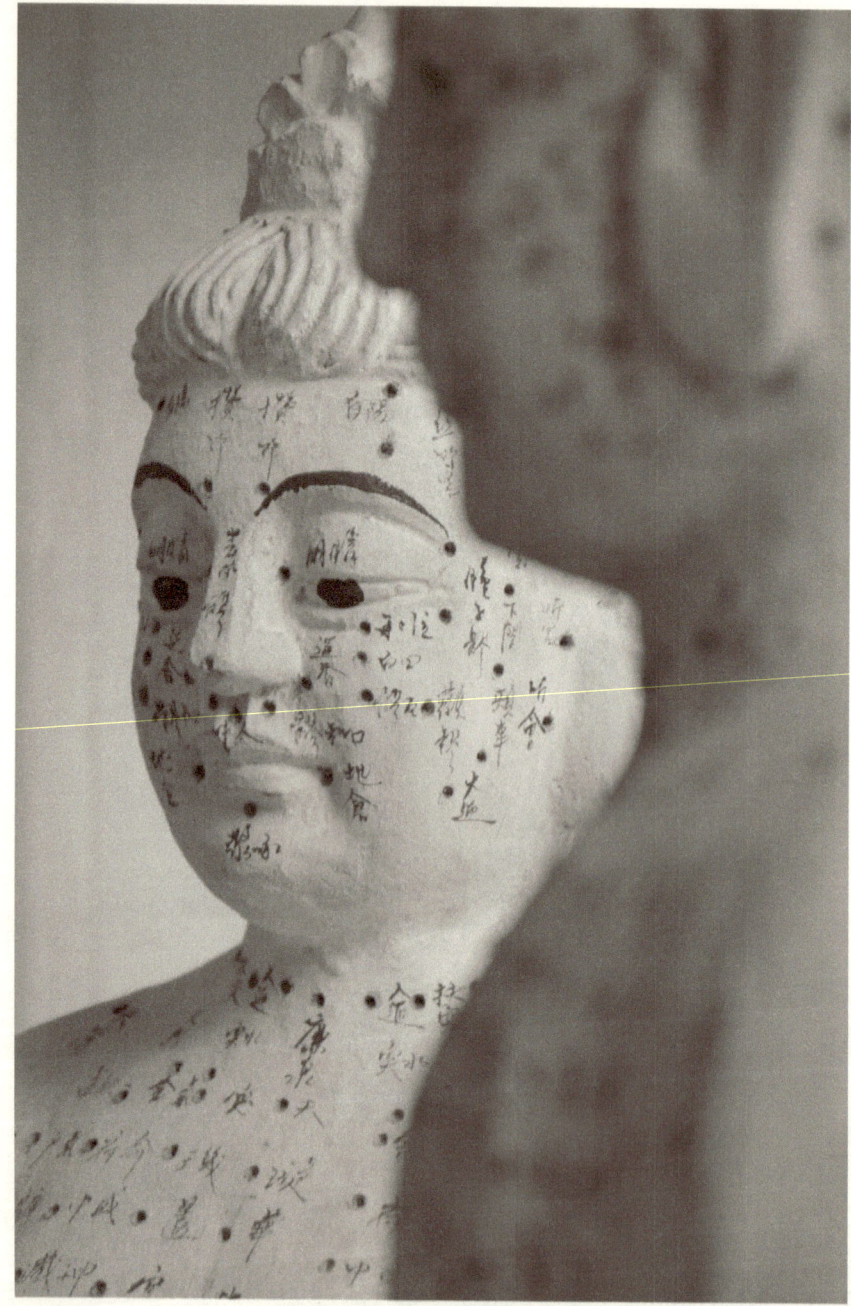

Figure 2.2 The art of acupuncture. Credit: Matthias Frank.

THE BODY IS CULTURE

1. Root Chakra (Muladhara): Stability and grounding.
2. Sacral Chakra (Svadhisthana): Creativity and emotions.
3. Solar Plexus Chakra (Manipura): Confidence and willpower.
4. Heart Chakra (Anahata): Love and compassion.
5. Throat Chakra (Vishuddha): Communication and self-expression.
6. Third Eye Chakra (Ajna): Intuition and insight.
7. Crown Chakra (Sahasrara): Spiritual connection and enlightenment (Figure 2.3).

The anatomist in our round table finds this whole thing strange, maybe laughable. But you practice yoga, and you really sense these energy centers. They aren't merely conceptual; they're sensorial, visible to you and to others, vital, wonderful. And it's wonderful to have a system and a vocabulary to organize and clarify these vital sensations. Someone says, "It's crazy to believe in chakras." Someone else says, "It's crazy not to believe in chakras."

Now it's the turn of our imaginary mystic, who goes by the name and pronoun Ze. I'd like to channel Ze and speak in Ze's style, which is brief and epigrammatic, incomprehensible but compelling.

> Latin, Chinese, and Sanskrit are such musical languages. The body is the many bodies, and the body is also the mind, and the mind is the many minds. On my way here I bumped into a black cat in the back alley. We hissed at each other.

Figure 2.3 The art of chakras. Credit: Gerd Altmann.

Figure 2.4 The art of tattoos. Credit: Anonymous via Pixabay.

Ze can't stop laughing, and I don't know what Ze's thinking anymore. I'm not dismissing Ze. On the contrary, I think Ze is on to something deeply meaningful, which can only be articulated in seemingly incoherent statements—that is, incoherent to other ways of thinking, but perfectly clear to Ze. In Ze's worldview, the laughing fit is an integral part of the discourse, the analysis, the conceptualizing.

Who are you? It's not a banal question. What culture has shaped you? What are the intellectual and emotional forces passing through you and helping or hindering you? What is your native tongue? I don't mean English and French; I mean the concepts behind your behaviors in daily life and in your music making. Your native tongue might be Anatomy, or it might be Chakras. Your vocabulary may emphasize bones or meridians. Your music making may emphasize an anatomically based technique, perhaps called *biomechanics*; or a mystically based interpretation, perhaps called *devotion*. Your culture doesn't have to be exclusive. It's perfectly possible to integrate multiple vocabularies, the basics of biomechanics and the basics of devotion. Ze really is on to something: the body is the many bodies, and the body is also the mind, and the mind is the many minds (Figures 2.4 and 2.5).

Figure 2.5 Reaching for the sun. Credit: John Hain.

Allowed, Forbidden

I grew up in São Paulo, Brazil. I was an awkward child and adolescent. I had a rich inner life, I excelled at academic subjects, I had a sense of humor and some talent for expressing myself and for offering remarks and insights (plus teases and provocations and harsh judgments) to other people. But I was as athletic as a deflated volleyball stuck in wet sand.

My late mother had a soft spot for me—for the whole of me, for the tender heart with a good vocabulary and the awkward body with the twisted ankle. I left Brazil when I was 19 years old to go study music in the United States. My life took some interesting turns: I started taking lessons in the Alexander Technique and practicing aikido. During one school vacation, back at home in Brazil, I was giving my younger brother a few hints regarding exercise that I had half-gathered from my bumbling efforts in the Alexander Technique and in aikido. Listening to our conversation, at some point my mother asked me, "Since when are you an expert in sports?" She seemed confused. The child for whom she had a soft spot, her deflated volleyball, her little hermit? She was having a hard time accepting my incipient transformation, and I sensed that she preferred the hermit to the athlete. In our family, we were "people of the brain," to coin an expression. To become myself, I had to betray my family.

I once gave a few cello lessons to a woman, an amateur beginner. Her long nails made it difficult for her to articulate notes, play in tune, vibrate, and shift positions. And the difficulty made her quite frustrated. Yet her long nails were nonnegotiable: they were required of her femininity as she perceived it and as dictated by her social circle. You weren't a woman if you didn't have long nails. In fact, she didn't even think her nails were long. Measures are always relative. Other women had long nails; hers seemed short to her.

Hands, wrists, and fingers behave according to the culture in which you situate yourself (willingly or unwillingly, consciously or unconsciously). Floppy wrists aren't manly. Big shoulders aren't feminine. Handshakes: firm and clear! Hold the other person's hand, do two vigorous shakes with it: go up first, then down. Linger a fraction of a second too long, and you're implying intimacy. What's wrong with you?

Culture is forever talking to you, though not always in words (Figure 2.6).

The ultimate change, the last step in your self-growth, is to recognize your own culture, of which you're normally unaware, the culture that envelops you like a cocoon, and to undress yourself, as it were: to let go of aspects of your culture, or even of the basic tenets of your culture; to give up thinking and feeling that "this is how you were raised" as the justification for inertia and resistance; to raise yourself again in a new culture, formerly foreign. To become someone else; to abandon the personality of pain and to embrace the personality of freedom, of pleasure, of flow; to let go of the identification

Figure 2.6 Skills of manicure. Credit: Frauke Riether.

you may have with pain and disability, the pain that "makes you," the pain about which you have depths of feeling, untold memories, a stream of stories, arguments, a sort of theology. If pain is a god, you must become an atheist, at the risk of excommunication, if only from your own inner judge. But the excommunication may also involve other people: friends and family who have always known you in a state of pain and who might reject the stranger that you may be becoming.

In short, culture is a song of "allowed, forbidden." Inevitably, your individual life is also a song of "allowed, forbidden." Creative Health is a way of singing these songs with intelligence, alertness, sensitivity, and humor.

Touch Is Culture

The vocabulary of touch varies from culture to culture. In Brazil, greeting people with cheek-to-cheek kisses is more than normal; depending on context, it's expected and required. Attending a dinner party, you meet a few people for the first time. Two women will always do the cheek-to-cheek; a man and a woman will always do the cheek-to-cheek; two men will never do the cheek-to-cheek. The habit is deeply ingrained and essentially never examined or questioned. If you don't greet people with the cheek-to-cheek, you'll come across as aloof, cold, hostile, superior, foreign. In America, cheek-to-cheek between strangers is taboo. Do this at a dinner party, and you'll be seen as a molester, a predator. This, too, is deeply ingrained and charged with assumptions and judgments.

In many cultures, communication is both verbal and physical; people talk to one another at close range, often touching their listeners with their hands. Your interlocutor might use your arms and shoulders as a sort of percussion instrument, tapping you for connection, emphasis, and continuity. In other cultures, personal space is sacrosanct. Your interlocutor might wear an invisible shield announcing the limits of proximity. Once you capture the phenomenon in its complexity, you understand that hands speak and behave differently in different cultures.

From birth onward, your hands are trained to touch the other or not touch the other, to gesticulate in speech or not to gesticulate in speech, to reach out or to refrain from reaching out. This doesn't mean that a given culture is better or healthier than another culture; it means that you have ingrained cultural habits predetermining some of the behaviors that your hands are allowed or encouraged to display, and behaviors that you're discouraged and forbidden from displaying (Figures 2.7 and 2.8).

There are many cultures in which two men who are friends walk holding hands. Being symbolic of friendship and mutual appreciation, the

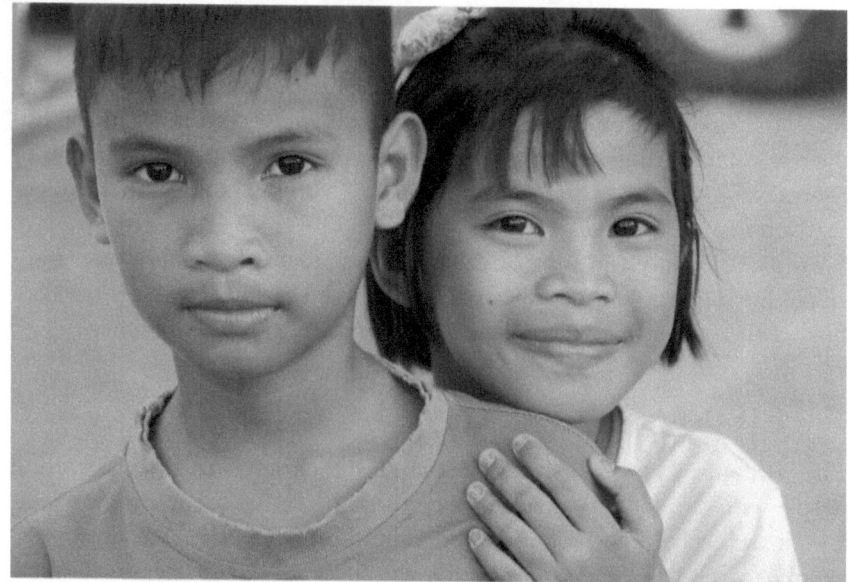

Figure 2.7 Touch of friendship. Credit: Dean Moriarty.

Figure 2.8 Touch of communication. Credit: Alicja.

handholding is unshakable, so to speak; it'd be extremely difficult for a man from the handholding culture to not hold hands with a dear friend. And there are cultures in which two men holding hands are the subject of derision, gossip, and assumptions, which some people confuse with indisputable truths: "Only those kinds of people do that kind of thing." What happens when the hand holder visits a non-hand holder friend, or more broadly when a taboo meets the opposite taboo? A high-placed Arab prince visits America for important diplomatic discussions, and he'll be seen with his old friend the American president walking hand-in-hand on the grounds of the White House. The American public, watching the news or reading a newspaper, will find it rather discomfiting, to use a euphemism. Truth be told, many Americans will be shocked and disgusted.

Your hands are part of the social discourse, forever dancing the dances of friendship, propriety, obligations, and taboos. Consciously or not, you might make fine distinctions between this person, whose hands you can shake for one second, and this other person, whose hands you must shake for two seconds but not three seconds, no, no. I had a French student for a year or so. She would knock, I would open the door and say "bonjour" with a smile, she would enter the room. One day she told me that she always felt uncomfortable arriving for her lesson because I didn't offer my hand for a handshake which, in her innermost being, was obligatory. The "bonjour" and the smile didn't compensate for my social breach.

Rings, Bracelets, Watches

The aesthetics of your hands are also culturally determined to some degree. Bracelets and rings are an integral part of some people's lives. You could feel completely naked if you left the house without the bracelets that you habitually wear. A wedding ring on the right ring finger is obligatory for certain social groups. If you don't wear a wedding ring, it can only mean that you aren't married! Wristwatches tell the time, but they also tell stories about the people wearing them. They may be displays of masculinity or femininity; on your wrist you may wear a symbol of power, wealth, status, education, and social class. Someone might wear multiple rings and bracelets, plus a watch. In fact, someone may own a huge collection of rings, bracelets, and watches that are forever interacting in interesting displays of mood and creativity (Figure 2.9).

The accoutrements are an extension of the wrists and fingers, making them bigger, more prominent, more visible. Certain cultures allow and encourage men to wear multiple rings and bracelets; others forbid it. To the attentive mind, there's nothing banal about a bracelet on your wrist. Besides being a possible sociocultural marker, it also transforms the energy of your wrist

Figure 2.9 Hands of elegance. Credit: Karolina Grabowska.

and hand. And, by transforming their energy, it might also transform their behavior. The changes may be minuscule, but they're undeniable. Sometimes we see a video clip of a cat whose owner puts little socks on the cat's paws. And the cat goes completely crazy because those little socks are unnatural, a threat, a horror. The cat's reaction is an authentic response to the addition of an accoutrement to an extremity. It illustrates the potential effect of a peripheral accoutrement on the whole organism.

Let's imagine a stereotypical mafioso, like someone in a TV show. The big, expensive watch on his wrist signals power and danger; you don't want to mess around with a man who owns this watch and wears it. Now let's imagine that one morning the fellow forgets to put on his watch before leaving the house and going to take care of business. Our perception of his threatening nature will be inevitably transformed—a little or a lot.

Accoutrements alter the flow of energy, sometimes blocking it, sometimes enhancing it. Shoes on, shoes off: different energies. Socks on, socks off: different energies. Eyeglasses on, eyeglasses off: the wearer is transformed. Rings on, rings off; bracelets on, bracelets off; wristwatch on, wristwatch off: depending on your temperament and sensitivity, you become a different person (Figure 2.10).

Imagine that you like your wrists and fingers to remain free from accoutrements. You prefer to move unimpeded by constraints and distractions, and

Figure 2.10 Hands of ritual. Credit: Gaurav Kumar.

you dislike the bracelets' jiggly noises. Now imagine that for some reason you must wear a watch to play a concerto—maybe because of a sponsorship deal, or maybe because your loving partner made you a loving gift and, you know, there's no way out of the situation. Oh, how horrible, how unbearable! And yet, it's not impossible that you'll discover that the watch has a strange, beneficial effect on your playing. Either way, the General Law of Accoutrements states that there is and there must be a change in energy, perception, and behavior on account of an accoutrement or its absence.

For years you may have played the piano wearing a wristwatch and not thinking about it. One day you take the watch off and you're astounded at the difference in your sensations and emotions, also in your sounds, your dexterity, your ease at the piano. Then you ask yourself, "Why didn't I take the watch off decades ago?" It's not easy to be fully alert to habits, to cultural norms, to assumptions and judgments, to the hidden intentions driving behaviors of all types (Figure 2.11).

Rings, watches, bracelets, and every accoutrement worn on the wrists or fingers have symbolic and ritualistic powers. Ponder *The Ring of the Nibelung*, Richard Wagner's four-opera cycle centered on a cursed ring that grants dominion over the world. A cheap ring that you wear without thinking may not be as cursed or as powerful, but it manifests, in its own modest way, the archetype of Ring, or the idea of Ring. It's not difficult to hyperlink from that

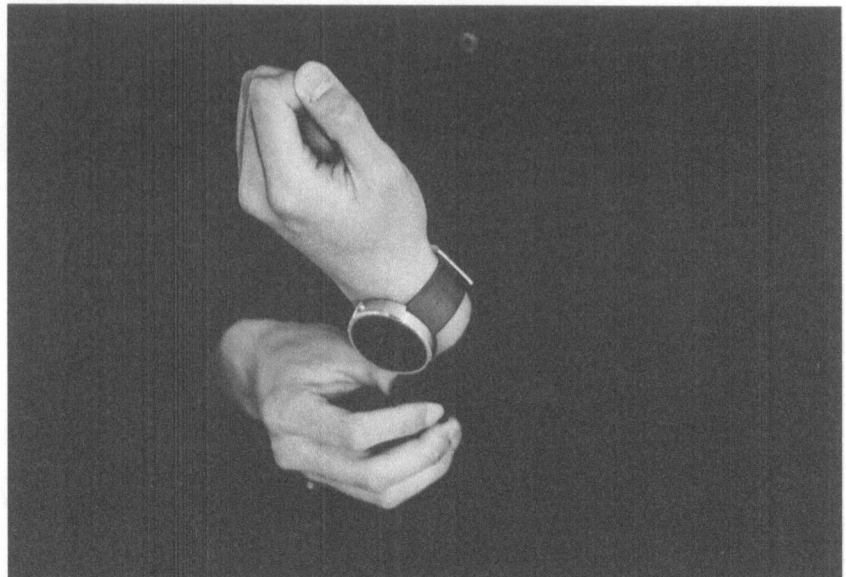

Figure 2.11 The power of watches. Credit: Pexels.

cheap ring of yours to countless other aspects of ring as idea: the incredible rings around Saturn, composed of billions of particles ranging in size from tiny grains of dust to chunks as large as mountains; the rings of criminals terrorizing a city or country; the ring of smoke blown in your face by a rebel without a cause; the rings in mathematics, showing up in cryptography and algebraic geometry; dozens and dozens of types of rings informing your life without you necessarily noticing their presence or their interaction.

Ring (that is, the archetype behind all rings) expresses circularity, cycle, circumscription (things are either inside the ring or outside it); Ring is a marker of space, delineating a territory; Ring talks to your senses and Ring talks to your unconscious. Listen to Ring, then decide if it helps you or hinders you to wear one or more rings, to wear them some of the time or nonstop, to wear them when you practice and when you perform.

The Mask

You may be gathering that I believe in archetypes, although I have a hard time explaining what I mean by it. For instance, there are dozens of types of rings, thousands and thousands of specific rings, millions and millions of ways of wearing rings; and behind all rings there is Ring, the deity (I say this informally, and sort of jokingly) that has offered us all the different rings and ways of interacting with rings.

The informality, the jokes hiding some big ideas, the contradictions are all part of Creative Health.

Let me introduce another poorly articulated archetype that I'm informally calling a deity: Mask. You wear a mask at a party, on Hallowe'en or elsewhere. For hygienic reasons, you wear a surgical mask in some settings. When skiing, you wear a balaclava to protect your face from the cold—and the balaclava is a mask, of course. Eyeglasses are a type of mask. A friend of yours wears glasses nonstop. One day you see the friend without the eyeglasses: naked, unmasked, utterly transformed—at least in your perception. It's an amazing phenomenon.

Makeup is a mask. War paint is a mask. But you don't have to wear a mask to have a mask on; you can put on a formal face, which is a mask of thoughts and emotions; you can pull a long face; you can put on dozens of varied face masks without wearing a physical object.

The more you think about Mask, the more you see its manifestations all around you, in your very person, your very existence. Broaden the concept, and you'll see clothes as Mask; words as Mask; political initiatives as Mask; digital identities as Mask. What you wear on stage to give a performance is Mask, regardless of the specific clothes: tails and tuxedos are Mask, gowns are Mask, T-shirts are Mask.

It's transformative to put a mask on, and it's transformative to take it off. Masks are *always* transformative, sometimes just a little bit, sometimes a tremendous amount.

But right now, I'm trying to get us to think about cultures in which it's either acceptable or obligatory for you to wear Mask on your hands, in the form of one or more tattoos or one or more henna designs (Figures 2.12, 2.13, and 2.14).

Henna, a natural dye from the henna plant, is used across many cultures (including India, North Africa, and the Middle East) to adorn hands and feet with intricate designs celebrating love, protecting against the evil eye, attracting prosperity, encouraging fertility, and bringing blessings. Spirituality, art, beauty, ritual, community, and other existential dimensions are reflected and strengthened by the simple or elaborate covering of hands with henna patterns. And as you and I have determined together, Mask is transformative. Hennaed hands think differently, feel differently, and behave differently.

Let's stretch our game of Archetype and say that henna is a manifestation of Henna. Little kids sometimes get temporary tattoos on their tender little hands, and the kids are delighted, transported, or excited on account of their encounter with a cultural and creative resource with identity-changing capabilities. The temporary tattoos aren't literally henna, but metaphorically they're Henna.

Figure 2.12 Tattooed upper limb. Credit: Photorama.

We'll be little kids. Instead of tattoos, we'll draw on our hands. Here's the exercise.

1. Gather a set of water-soluble markers, the type that is safe for kids to play with. How many colors? Let the kid decide. I want 12 colors.
2. Use your dominant hand to make designs on the nondominant hand. What kind of designs? Let the kid decide. I'm going to draw a funny monster face on my palm, big ears and horns, and maybe a hat along the fingers, and another face on the back of my hand. It's going to be Good Ol' Two-Face, wizard and witch, princess and prince, Jack and Jill, my good side and my bad side, the sun and the moon.
3. Does it have to be skillfully drawn and worthy of art school? Let the kid decide. I'll do my best to be clever and inventive, and if it turns out messy I'll laugh at myself. Or I'll wash the ink off my hands and start all over again.
4. Does it have to be sort of figurative, like a face? Let the kid decide. Maybe I'll do hieroglyphs or runes or just a thousand dots.
5. Is it going to tickle? Yes. Will you enjoy the tickling? Let the kid decide. Are you going to go on a head trip? Are you going to talk and sing to yourself? Are you going to be a little afraid and very excited? Let the kid decide. I'll go on a head trip for sure.

Figure 2.13 Heart of henna. Credit: u_twa0qr4415.

Figure 2.14 Henna and bangles. Credit: Irshad Rahimbux.

Figure 2.15 Hands as palimpsest. Credit: Lisa Runnels.

6. Do you have to cover the entire hand, front and back, the whole of each finger from base to fingertip, plus a bracelet around the wrist? Let the kid decide. I'm going to cover every pore of my hand, plus a bracelet around the wrist.
7. Do you have to use your nondominant hand to repeat the process and draw on your dominant hand? Let the kid decide. Yes, of course! Do the two hands have to have identical drawings? Let the kid decide. Nah. Will you show everyone in the house your handiwork, hahaha? Let the kid decide. I'll be excited and proud; I'll laugh at myself, and I won't want to wash my hands ever again.
8. Do you have to play your instrument with your hands completely covered in strange marks and drawings? Let the kid decide. I want to. Do you have to convince your chamber music partners to join in the fun? Let the kid decide. If you don't draw Mask on your hands, I'm not your friend anymore.
9. Do you have to perform a recital or a gig or an audition wearing Henna on your Hands? Let the kid decide. I feel so good; I'll play so well, the public will be surprised and shocked; everyone will take photos and post them on social media. It's exactly what I want.
10. Does this make any sense at all? Let the kid decide (Figure 2.15).

Chapter 3

DISCOVERY AND REDISCOVERY

You make music, and your hands, wrists, and fingers are exceedingly important to you. This is natural and inevitable, but also paradoxical: you *must think* about your hands, wrists, and fingers; and you also *must stop thinking* about your hands, wrists, and fingers. Fretting, worrying, and obsessing about your hands isn't good. But sensing, celebrating, and enjoying your hands is good! Concentrating on your hands at the risk of not being attentive to the music itself isn't good. But allowing the hands to respond to a musical stimulus is very, very good!

Let's see what we can do about it.

Newborn, baby, toddler, kindergartner: the child is forever making discoveries. Everything is new, everything is worthy of the child's attention, everything is fascinating and wonderful—unless it's incomprehensible and terrifying. A toddler notices her shadow for the first time, and she panics: What is this horrible thing that's following me around? Is it trying to kill me? Discovery is an exciting energy like no other. Our job is to live in wonderment, with the excitement of discovery not hampered by habit, routine, inattention, cynicism, or any of those troublesome adult emotions that are foreign to the baby.

Here's the exercise: watch the hands of babies and young children at play.

Tender little fingers, agile, intelligent, sometimes already structured: a baby with "pianist's hands," space between the fingers, curved fingers ready to approach the keyboard. Child and pencil, child and recorder, child and tricycle, child holding the hand of another child, child holding your hand ... looking and marveling could become a full-time occupation (Figure 3.1).

We tend to look at things through a filter of feelings, memories, stories, fears, likes and dislikes, assumptions, and judgments. This means that we don't really look at a thing, but at a foggy screen upon which we project our thoughts and feelings about that thing. This applies not only to our hands but also to our musical instruments, our homes, our friends and frenemies, works of art, trees, animals, everything.

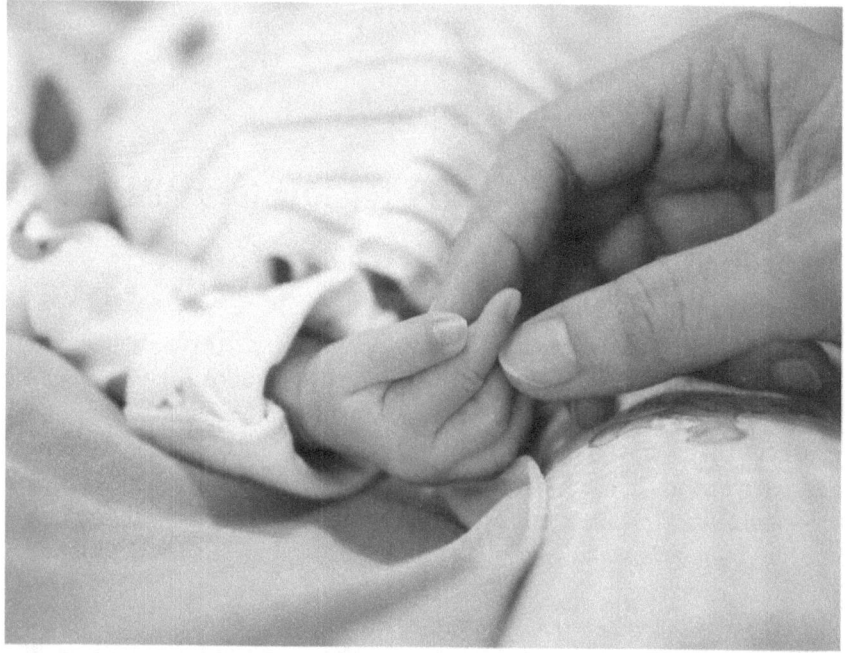

Figure 3.1 Enchantment of birth. Credit: Pexels.

Here's the exercise: look at your hands. What's the soundscape playing in your mind? Who's saying what, and to whom?

The average museumgoer looks at a work of art for 15 seconds before moving on to the next one. We all tend to look distractedly and not see. Lingering on an image, object, landscape, or person takes practice and discipline. And seeing, which is different from simply lingering, takes even more practice and discipline.

Here's the exercise: choose something to look at and linger over the act of looking.

Looking at your computer screen or smartphone doesn't count. Sunsets, façades, vases and flowers, cats, birds—there are so many choices. If you're an art lover, pick a favorite work of art and park yourself in front of it for 30 minutes. Or pick a painting that you don't like and look at it until you really see it. Schedule multiple sessions and lengthen the duration of the sessions over the days and weeks.

Looking at a beautiful work of art for a long time is relatively easy. Looking at your own self, or at a part of yourself, tends to be harder.

Here's the exercise: look at your hands again (Figure 3.2).

Figure 3.2 Enchantment of discovery. Credit: Julia Sezemova.

Set a time: 60 seconds, for instance. Or run a stopwatch and check to see how long you can look at your hands before you turn your attention away. Look at your hands, lovingly or dispassionately, for as long as you can and without worrying about the clock. Ponder their form and their proportions, the relationship between the palms and the fingers, the variety of finger shapes, the marvelous thumbs so unlike the other fingers. Look at your hands as you move them, open and close them, expand and shrink them. Watch a puppet play, in which your two naked hands perform the leading roles.

The size of hands, wrists, and fingers is always relative. One measuring stick might be the size of the whole body. Seemingly big hands might not appear so big if they belong to a tall and broad-framed person. Another measuring stick is *other people*. Most of us have delighted in placing our hands palm-to-palm against someone else's hands and marveling at the contrast.

Here's the exercise: go palm-to-palm with friends, family members, colleagues, and students. Go palm-to-palm with a willing young child.

Imagine a short person with very large hands. You might find the hands strange or laughable or disturbing, because "the proportions are all wrong." Those hands are inviting you to revise your assumptions about sizes and proportions, and above all your habits regarding right and wrong.

Here's the exercise: go to a fine museum and look at the proportions of arms, hands, wrists, and fingers depicted in paintings and sculptures. If you don't like museums or if you don't have easy access to one, do your study on the Internet. A committed study of depicted hands will broaden your perspective on proportions.

Hands are a bit like cats: they can make themselves bigger and smaller, according to need. Let's say you're feeling lazy about unbuttoning a shirt sleeve while getting dressed. Then you shrink your hand and push it through the tight cuff. Now let's say you want to protect your face from an incoming spurt of water. Then you open your hands as wide as possible and use them as a barrier.

Here's the exercise: stop what you're doing right now, and spend time making your hands bigger and smaller, bigger still and smaller still, absurdly big and absurdly small (Figure 3.3).

In the history of music, there have been all sorts of combinations: someone with arms too long to play the violin comfortably, someone else with the same length of arms finding a necessary compromise, and a third person with the same length of arms completely comfortable with the violin.

Here's the exercise: go to an orchestra concert and watch the eighty or hundred musicians as a study in size and proportions.

You can't isolate physicality from the whole person and his or her context: temperament, talent, training; aesthetics, family dynamics, sociocultural

DISCOVERY AND REDISCOVERY 43

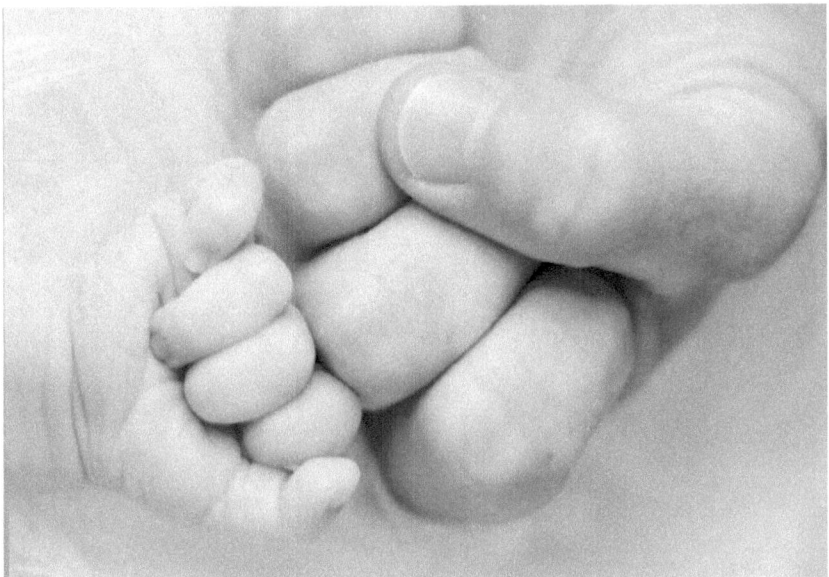

Figure 3.3 Enchantment of comparison. Credit: Anonymous via Pixabay.

background. Every time you wish to zero in on a dimension such as a hand or finger, remember (and make yourself remember) that any dimension in isolation is an abstraction. If you understand that you're abstracting, you own the dimension.

Here's the exercise: look at your hands intently, then let your mind zoom out gradually: hands, hands and arms, hands and arms and the whole body, hands and arms and the whole body and family history, hands and arms and the whole body and family history and sociocultural background (Figure 3.4).

Big hands with stiff joints are very different from big hands with soft joints. Big skinny bones are very different from big fleshy bones. Thick, flexible wrists are very different from thin, flexible wrists. Hands, wrists, and fingers are built of many characteristics in dynamic interaction, rendering individual characteristics relatively unimportant.

Here's the exercise: look at your hands, palpate them, wrap a hand around the other wrist, pull on your fingers. Instead of analyzing their characteristics, just handle your hands in sheer sensorial pleasure.

You meet someone whose handshake seems awkward. The person is reserved or fussy or distant, the hand isn't fully offered, the hand is protected by an invisible sheath. "Strange hands." A few years later you meet this person again. The hand is more welcoming, more available, less protected. "Unrecognizable hands." The principle is general: objectivity and

Figure 3.4 Enchantment of care. Credit: Pexels.

absolutes don't apply to the human dimension. "My hands are like this, have always been like this, will always be like this." No, not true! "My hands live and breathe, my hands have thoughts and emotions, my hands change and grow, my hands have moods, to some people my hands show their tender side, to others my hands are hostile; when I'm comfortable, my hands behave in a certain way; if I'm half-asleep, irritated, or angry, my hands behave in another way. I change, and my hands change." Yes, true!

Here's the exercise: zoom out of the current moment and ponder the unfolding of your life over a few years or a decade or longer. In what ways have you changed? To what degree are you changeable? How have your hands changed over time?

In Praise of Vocabulary

Decades ago, I gave a friend a little compliment: I called him brilliant. He thought about it for a moment, then disagreed with me. "I don't think I'm brilliant, but I do think I'm astute." He was right. One can be clever, intelligent, astute, brilliant, witty, insightful, or canny, among many qualities. One can also have a combination of these qualities. The main thing, though, is that "brilliant" and "astute" are different, and it's beneficial to be able to tell them apart and to have words to articulate the distinction.

"Vocabulary" comes from the same root as "voice." To have a rich vocabulary is to have a rich way of voicing your thoughts and feelings. It's wonderful to know the vocabulary of music, which is vast; it's wonderful to be comfortable with technical words and with the names of musical phenomena; it's wonderful not to be afraid of the hemiola, the submediant, and the double-augmented descending sixth; and it's wonderful to commit to the steady expansion of the vocabulary that underpins your voice. Don't worry; I'm not about to interrogate you on the submediant or the hemiola. Here I'm inviting you to develop rich ways of describing hands, wrists, and fingers; to observe fine distinctions among many types of hands; to be able to describe these distinctions; and to become able to celebrate the remarkable diversity of hands, the better to celebrate the uniqueness of your own hands.

Bones, big and strong; slim and bristle; long and twisted; prominent, as if poking out of the hands; not prominent, as if hiding under layers of skin and fat. Bones of an arm wrestler, bones of a Russian ballerina, bones of a Cuban dancer, bones of a giant, bones so long that there isn't enough flesh to envelop the bones. Notice that we're mixing different ways of talking about bones, passing from the more or less anatomical to the more or less imaginative.

What are your knuckles like? Bony, knobby, angular; calloused, prominent, smooth; rough, wrinkled, swollen; defined, chiseled, fleshy; bulging, scarred, veined; compact, tapered, rigid; blistered, tender, weathered; pale, reddened, bruised; arthritic, flexible, creased; tough, slim, robust. Read this list out loud while caressing your own knuckles. Or take a water-soluble marker and, while reading the list out loud, draw points and crosses on your knuckles, going back and forth, reciting, chanting, drawing, laughing. The idea is to have a plethora of thoughts, feelings, images, and metaphors of knuckles at the forefront of your awareness.

The word itself has many cousins, in that zone of English where German and Dutch are always hobnobbing: knob, knock, knuckle, knoll, knurl; knee, knife, knout. Just looking at these words will play a trick on your brain. Then you'll develop a brain tic: every time you think of your knuckles, your brain will flood with strange letters and sounds; every time you use a knife, you'll notice your knuckles; every time you bend your knees, you'll start scatting an onomatopoeic nonsense song: knickknack knickerbocker, put your knickers in the locker (Figure 3.5).

Knuckle sandwich, a punch; a white-knuckle ride, intense and scary; a bareknuckle fight, and sometimes the expression would be appropriate to describe certain ways of playing the piano or the drums or any other instrument. You might knuckle down for a few days to prepare for an audition or to learn a new score. Don't show up unprepared for your solfège lesson with Madame Dieudonné, or she'll rap your knuckles, you knucklehead!

Figure 3.5 Power of knuckles. Credit: Steward Masweneng.

Fingers, slim or thick, long or elongated, twisted or crooked, spongy, elastic, wiry, elegant, inelegant, fleshy and short, fleshy and long, fleshy and graceful, so fleshy that you feel queasy just looking at them. Red alert! You've just passed from observing to reacting, from observing to judging.

Descriptive adjectives are different from compliments and insults. The fingers are long, relative to the size of the palm: this is descriptive. The most gorgeous long fingers: a compliment, arising from your emotions when seeing the fingers. This is the realm of head trips, storytelling, and judgments good and bad. I'm not saying you shouldn't compliment people on their most gorgeous long fingers; I'm saying that it's useful to make a distinction between descriptive vocabulary, which talks about the fingers, and evaluative vocabulary, which talks about your emotions regarding the fingers. It's good to have emotions; it's not so good to use evaluative vocabulary when you really mean to employ descriptive vocabulary. And when emotions run negative—for instance, when you're tempted to speak ill of your own hands—it becomes urgent to shift the vocabulary from evaluative to descriptive.

Nails might be shiny, dull, glossy, matte, opaque, transparent, smooth, ridged, discolored, even, or uneven. They may appear to be healthy, brittle, strong, weak, flaky, chipped, split, peeling, damaged, hardened, thickened, or thin. Their shape might be oval, round, square, almond-shaped, pointed, flat, curved, or asymmetrical. They may appear overgrown, trimmed, polished, unkempt, or manicured. Their texture might be smooth, rough, grooved, bumpy, soft, or calloused. Your nails aren't my nails; and your nails right now aren't your nails of two days from now.

DISCOVERY AND REDISCOVERY

Look at your nails and use the descriptive vocabulary to help you see and understand your nails, their current state, their function in your daily life and in your music practice, their role in your creative life. Your nails are a sort of self-portrait. Proof of it is that no one else has nails exactly like yours.

It's interesting that the word "nail" means two different things: "A hard, keratinous covering on the tips of fingers and toes, protecting the digits and aiding in grasping" and "a slender, pointed metal spike used for fastening or securing objects together, typically driven in with a hammer." A fool might confuse the two and hurt someone in the process, but an imaginative creative type might purposefully confuse the two and enjoy the enhanced alertness that results from the confusion.

Nails may be as sharp as weapons. You might be afraid of nails scratching off your eyes or digging into your skin and drawing blood. That would make for a nail-biter of a movie, wouldn't it? Alternatively, you can sit holding your lover's hands and endlessly caress the points of his or her incredible, magical claws. I mean, nails—the incredible painted nails, the incredible melding of biology and art at the end of fingertips.

Nails aren't claws; nails are just like claws; both statements are true. It's up to you to decide what to do with the idea that your nails are claws. I wouldn't want to predetermine your choices, but to see yourself as an animal with claws might give you a feeling of power and pleasure; it might get you to take good care of your nails; it might lead you to play your instrument with just a bit of extra ingenuity. Your neighborhood might be chock-a-block with nail salons, and you might be tempted to judge their customers a little harshly. But in the continuum between careless indifference to one's nails and obsessive narcissism with one's nails, there may be a place for you to become healthily nail-oriented, to coin an expression (Figures 3.6, 3.7, 3.8, and 3.9).

The First Time

There is a first time when the baby notices its own fingers, its own strange appendages that seem to have an independent will, wow! The first time when the baby stands on two legs, wow! The first independent steps, wow! The first complete sentences, wow!

It's said that you learn more things in the first six years of your life than in the rest of your whole life. It doesn't matter if the statement is scientifically right or wrong. We'll interpret it for our own purposes and say that learning is deeply energized by its association with discovery.

For our overall well-being and for the creative health of our hands, wrists, and fingers, our challenge is to live permanently with the same sense of discovery and pleasure that we have when we do something for the first time.

Figure 3.6 Power of claws. Credit: Artur Pawlak.

Figure 3.7 Beauty of claws. Credit: Rethinktwice.

Figure 3.8 Claws in context. Credit: G.C.

Figure 3.9 Extravagant claws. Credit: G.C.

One tool is to become alert to the phenomenon, which we'll call First-Time with capitals and a hyphen. First-Time is innocent, curious, adventurous. First-Time is fascinated, puzzled, delighted. First-Time takes risks, and sometimes First-Time gets hurt. First-Time is forever imprinting lively information upon its sweet, flexible First-Time brain. First-Time is drunk with first times, and First-Time never runs out of first times.

Make a list of things you've done, said, felt, or thought for the first time. The list can include the most ordinary things from daily life—things that only became ordinary because their first-time-ever got dissipated in memory and, sometimes, in indifference or cynicism. And the list can include more special things and events: the first time riding a plane, the first kiss, the first heartbreak (Figure 3.10).

Make a list of the first times in your musical life. I remember the jolt of recognition when I first understood the difference between D major and D minor. I was eight years old. I remember my very first performance: a little piece for recorder and piano, which I played at a Christmas event at one of the places where my father worked. It was nerve-racking and mind-blowing. I was nine years old. I remember my first cello lesson; nerve-racking and mind-blowing. First purchase of the score of J. S. Bach's Suites for solo cello; nerve-racking and mind-blowing. First time when my brother sat on my cello bow and broke it in half; actually, the first and only time; very, very mind-blowing and nerve-racking. My list of first-time musical events contains hundreds and hundreds of items—so many items that I consider the list infinite. Today and yesterday I did many things for the first time; tomorrow I'll do many things for the first time. I don't have to try to do those things; they arise naturally and inevitably from the simple reality of my being alive.

What about the first time of things involving your hands, wrists, and fingers? Memory is an intriguing human capability. It's tempting to call it flawed, but it only appears flawed to a strict left brain that prizes facts and measures. Let's say that there's a no-man's land between memory and invention, and let's say that it's good to be alert to this land and to occupy it willingly. When it's impossible to remember something (the first time you became aware of your hands), relax and make something up—something useful and amusing, strange, bizarre, marvelous; or something useless and banal; it doesn't matter, because exercising your memory-invention enhances your Creative Health and your musical life.

I used to forget the smell of floor wax in the stairways of my building, and when I came home from a trip, I was always struck by it. The smell itself was pleasant, but the feeling that I was being welcomed back was particularly heartwarming. The floor wax talked to me, and every time was the first time I heard the floor wax talk because I had forgotten the time before. First-Time

Figure 3.10 Wonderment. Credit: Sally Wynn.

Figure 3.11 Hands of commitment. Credit: Svklimkin.

isn't literal-minded; what counts is the feeling of first time, not the practicalities of it.

If remembering is a remarkable and ambiguous human capability, so is forgetting. It's good to forget the smell of floor wax and rediscover it; it's good to forget about a box of mementos in the attic and rediscover it; it's good to forget a musical composition you used to play in decades past and rediscover it. And it's good to forget your hands, wrists, and fingers, and to rediscover them again and again. "Oh how I love the smell of floor wax, oh how I love this photo of my older brother when he was three, oh how I love these incredible hands of mine!" (Figure 3.11).

Chapter 4

THE POWER OF STORY

Every language contains a wealth of metaphorical expressions involving the hands—as well as the wrists, the fingers, and other body parts. Here's a short sample of expressions about the hands:

> Give me a hand, raise your hand, the hand of God, call the handyman, those observations go hand in hand, all hands on deck, force someone's hand, you gotta hand it to her, a backhanded compliment, I live hand to mouth, things are getting out of hand, the judge employed a heavy hand, I know it like the back of my hand, in safe hands, hand in glove, I bought a secondhand shirt, my hands are tied, I wash my hands of this whole affair, "on the one hand [...] on the other hand [...]"

As these expressions attest, hands are deeply intertwined with the symbolic dimensions of existence, which are contained in the stories we tell ourselves. The idea of washing one's hands, for instance, is related to responsibility, guilt, remorse, and many other emotions. In some tellings of the biblical story (which may or may not be underpinned by historical events), Pontius Pilate washed his hands in front of the bloodthirsty crowd, indicating that he didn't consider himself responsible for the crucifixion of Christ: the matter now was in the hands of the crowd. Ever since, many millions of people have employed the expression many hundreds of millions of times. You don't need to know the original story or to believe in its historicity; the expression lives on, independently of Pontius Pilate, the crucifixion, and the Bible. Washing your hands is a banal act that isn't banal at all.

Sustained alertness to the symbols associated with the hands will charge gestures with a particular intelligence (Figure 4.1).

"Raise your hand!" The command indicates a physical gesture, but also the exhortation for you to express yourself, make yourself visible to the authorities and to your peers and mates, prepare yourself to make a choice and influence a decision, and so on. In a classroom full of first graders, the teacher asks everyone a question—about math, geography, language. Hands shoot up, eagerly competing for attention and validation, responding to the

Figure 4.1 Cleansing hands. Credit: Henryk Niestrój.

pleasure of learning and of showing off. The physicality of the stretched arm, the raised hand, and the spread palm with straight fingers is a response to a meaningful stimulus in a rich cultural context. The raised hand is a vital sign. Would you like your hands, wrists, and fingers to be healthy and strong? Respond meaningfully to a meaningful situation. Would you like to practice and master the art of healthy and strong hands? Respond meaningfully to a thousand meaningful situations (Figure 4.2).

Your hands symbolize responsibility, guilt, shame; cleansing and healing; decision-making and choice making; reaching out, sharing, touching others; the power of love and intimacy; the power of insulting, of fighting and hurting. The symbolic charge of your hands is, in fact, enormous. As you take your violin and your bow in your hands, you express the totality of your existence in gesture and sound; as you slice a tomato in your kitchen, the totality of your existence in gesture and nourishment; as you type at the computer, the totality of your existence in gesture and intellectual expression. In their movements, in their behaviors, and in their latent capabilities, the hands, wrists, and fingers are forever manifesting the totality of your existence.

Here's an exercise. Make your own list of words and expressions related to the hands, wrists, and fingers. You probably know songs and poems, or poem fragments, that involve the hands. Sing the songs, declaim the poems. Write the expressions down. Allow yourself to create new words and expressions. Get a few friends to do the exercise with you. Encourage a little competitiveness

Figure 4.2 Raising a hand. Credit: Indus International School, Bangalore.

to see who comes up with the most extravagant and absurd expressions. The words might come out in the form of puns, short poems, ditties, songs. Every time you enter an expression into your catalog, playact a little choreography inspired by the expression. "Raise your hand!" Story, joke, choreography. "Hands down, the worst president in history." Story, joke, choreography. This helps you embody the information and make it ready for practical use in the future.

Telling Stories

Here's a more involved exercise. Practice it with friends and family members, perhaps over drinks or at dinner. If you do it by yourself, consider writing your thoughts down in a journal. You'll tell four types of stories about your hands, though your stories are likely to spill over the limits of each story type.

Introduce your hands

Show us your hands and describe them to us. Tell us how they're built, how fleshy or how bony, how large or small, how beautiful and how elegant, how rough and how smooth, how clever and how clumsy. Tell us if you're right-handed or left-handed, or perhaps ambidextrous (Figure 4.3).

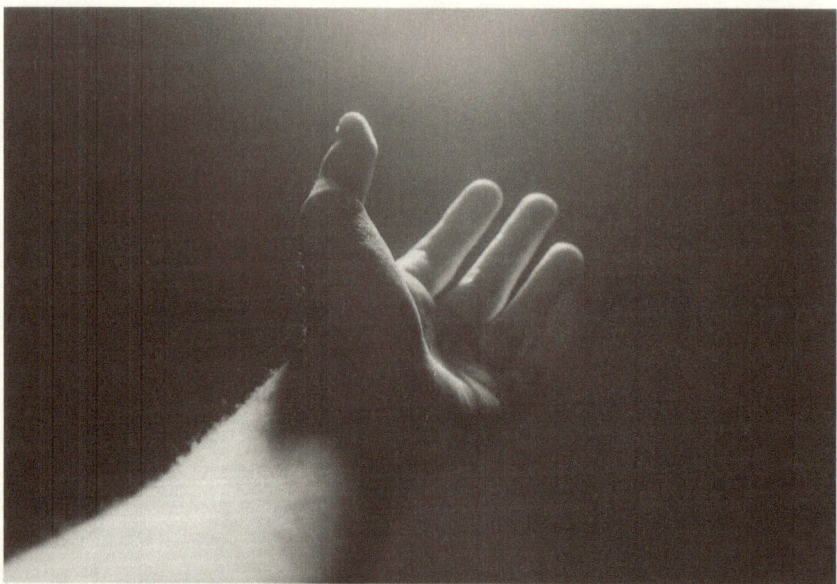

Figure 4.3 Reaching for the light. Credit: Anonymous via Pixabay.

This exercise is a meditation on distance and objectivity. Someone might say, "My hands are big for a person of my size, the palms broad, the fingers long and fleshy except for the little finger, which is much shorter than usual." That's a technical description. Suppose you now say, "All my life I've hated my hands." Then you've turned away from technical description and toward emotions and judgments. It's possible that you aren't looking at your hands as hands in themselves, but that you're projecting an image of self-doubt on a screen that sort of coincides with your hands.

"I see my hands; they look like this to me; my hands feel like this to me; I have these emotions about my hands." Other people looking at your hands will almost certainly see them in a different light. They may have strong feelings about your hands, or feelings about their own hands triggered by what they see in yours. "Oh, your hands are so long and elegant! Mine are squat and rough." Now your hands are affecting how other people feel. Your first-person hands live a parallel life in second-person and third-person points of view. Allow your fan club to admire your hands, then join the club and admire them yourself.

Strong feelings, attraction, disgust, appreciation, respect; callouses, nails, nail biting, thumb sucking; pleasure and shame. "Look at my nails! Don't look at my nails!" Thousands and thousands of memories regarding the hands and fingers, some memories self-contained as distinct moments in time, other memories a vague amalgamation of many experiences. Your hands are so big and broad that it's difficult to buy nice-fitting gloves for them. Your hands are tight, and they're so small, omigod your hands are tiny. How can you even play the freakin' viola?

It really isn't easy to be dispassionate about our own selves. But you'd learn a lot by engaging in this process of distancing. To give you an example, early on I had a difficult relationship with my cello, on account of my fears and blockages, my misplaced aspirations, my family history. And I was fused with my cello, so to speak; my feelings lived in the cello, emanated from the cello, spoke and sang through the cello. This is the "Mething Phenomenon," in which you're fused with a thing (or a person or an idea).

Over the decades, I did a lot of work to separate the cello from my inner self: I was me; the cello was the cello. In time my hesitations and confusions dissipated, and I started adoring my cello, that incredible, wonderful, perfect instrument who speaks and sings so beautifully. Again I became one with the cello; I am the perfect instrument who speaks and sings so beautifully. This is the return of the "Mething Phenomenon," now transformed (Figure 4.4).

By nature, human beings are full of asymmetries. Asymmetries can be so pronounced as to be problematic; for instance, a leg much shorter than the other creates postural imbalances with painful consequences. "Geography

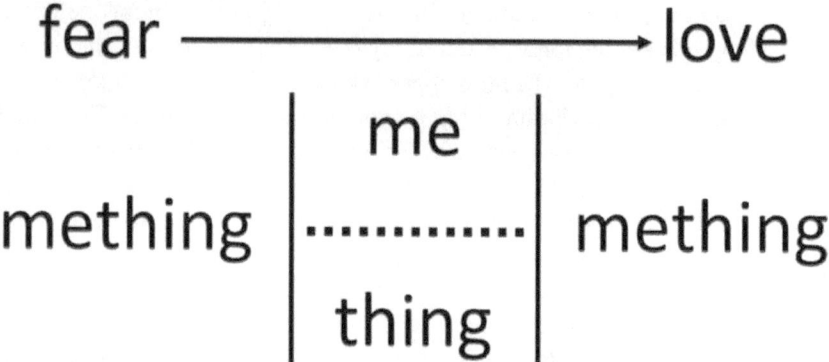

Figure 4.4 From fear to love. Credit: ©Pedro de Alcantara.

is destiny," Napoleon famously said; Russia's destiny, for instance, isn't Guatemala's destiny. We'll take the principle behind his saying and tweak it for our purposes: "Asymmetry is destiny." Your asymmetries play a role in your life, making you less like *this* and more like *that*, and contributing an important dimension to your existence. Asymmetries aren't limited to shapes and sizes. They involve capabilities, brain functions, psychomotor skills, habits, and preferences. It doesn't matter what instrument you play, or if you're a conductor or a singer: music making is inherently asymmetrical. Holding a flute or a violin, for instance, is an asymmetrical endeavor.

List the asymmetries in your body, from head to toe. List the asymmetries built into your musical instrument, for instance, the placement of the soundpost inside the cello or the crossed strings inside a grand piano. List the asymmetries of concert life, for instance, in how an ensemble occupies the stage. Map out asymmetries, and you'll create an interesting and enriching view of life.

The asymmetries between the left and right hands merit attention.

When I first moved to Paris, I lived in an apartment building with a concierge who had grown up in Portugal. From time to time we chatted in our shared native tongue. One day, she noticed me writing something with my left (and dominant) hand. She told me that she too was born left-handed, but when she was growing up, her parents and teachers would tie her left hand behind her back and force her to learn how to write with her right hand. The left hand was considered a dark and devilish thing. Writing with it was a perversion, which her culture had turned into a taboo. After she moved to France, there was a first time when she saw someone write with their left hand. She told me that she threw up when she saw it. She didn't tell me why, but I can easily imagine two reasons: she was witnessing a horrible taboo; and

Figure 4.5 Left-handed daemon. Credit: Andreas.

she was possibly understanding, viscerally, that she had been the victim of an abusive and superstitious cultural tradition (Figure 4.5).

A pianist might find a technical indication on a piano score, indicating in Italian that certain notes should be played with the left hand: "mano sinistra." In French, the word "sinistre" means "contrary, false, unfavorable, to the left." The Italian and French words come from the Latin "sinister," which means "left, to the left side," in opposition to "dexter," which refers to "readiness, skillfulness, prosperity," and which also means "right hand."

Simplifying it, the right hand is good (and "right"), the left hand is evil. If you're awkward and tactless, you're gauche (which is another French word for "left"). If you receive a left-handed compliment, you're being insulted. And if you have two left feet, you can't dance to save your life. But if you're a lefty in baseball or tennis, you may hold some strategic advantages over your right-handed adversaries.

Accidents, hurts, medical procedures

Daily life entails threats to your hands, wrists, and fingers: paper cuts, kitchen mishaps, overtrimmed nails that distract and bug you. An accidental hammer blow is made worse by self-reproach: "It hurts; I'm such an idiot." Dog bites, cat scratches, infections, Band-Aids, mercurochrome: your hands are a repository of events rich with sensations and emotions. Let's suppose you broke an arm when you were young. You received attention from doctors, nurses, parents, and siblings. Friends signed your plaster cast with names, hearts, arrows, doodles, and messages of love. The arm healed well, and the ordeal evolved into a cherished memory—a life-affirming tale of breaking and mending.

Tell these stories to yourself, to friends and family. The verb "tell" comes from an ancient root meaning "to speak, talk, say; count, number, compute; think, consider, reckon." Your stories can be modest or ambitious; it doesn't matter. For our purposes, a story about a paper cut is pertinent in its own way.

Let me tell you about the day the door slammed shut and caught my finger, at the hotel where my mother was staying while visiting me. It was 1983. I was finishing my studies at Yale School of Music in New Haven, and my mother came over from Brazil to attend my graduation recital. After the recital, I managed to take a couple of days off school to be with her in New York City. She was staying at the old Mayfair Hotel on Central Park. Her room had a heavy door with a strong spring mechanism. We were leaving the room when somehow the heavy door fell closed and caught my left ring finger.

It was a remarkable experience.

For various reasons, I reacted with a sort of detached distance, as if the event was happening to someone else. The physical displeasure was intense, but the emotions were low-key. My mother panicked. She immediately started blaming herself. "If I hadn't come over, this wouldn't have happened!" It was as if I was delegating the emotions to a third party, and the third party was out of control and making the situation more stressful.

I'll never forget the event, my mother's reactions, my reactions to her reactions, the song of pain that my brain composed and sang on the spot, the loss of my nail over a couple of weeks, the nail regrowth, the full recovery. And I'll never stop sensing the extremely faint echo of the whole story that I feel under the nail, at my fingertip, today, *now*. It's not painful at all, but there's some little tinge; the fingertip doesn't behave exactly like all the other fingertips. The spot at the fingertip plays a secret movie on a loop, featuring my late mother, the Mayfair Hotel in Central Park, Otto-Werner Müller, the conductor of the Yale Philharmonia, and my missed rehearsals while my finger healed. Plus many other secondary characters, extras with nonspeaking parts, weather, geography, history, architecture, and much else besides. New York City in 1983 was nothing like what it is today; a different world, a different movie set. "Mayfair Hotel, 1983: Fingertip and Mother." Indie movie written, directed, produced, and edited by Pedro de Alcantara. Original soundtrack by Pedro de Alcantara. In the role of the son: Pedro de Alcantara. In the role of the mother: Dulce Vieira Marcondes Machado. Special presentation, permanently available at your fingertips (Figure 4.6).

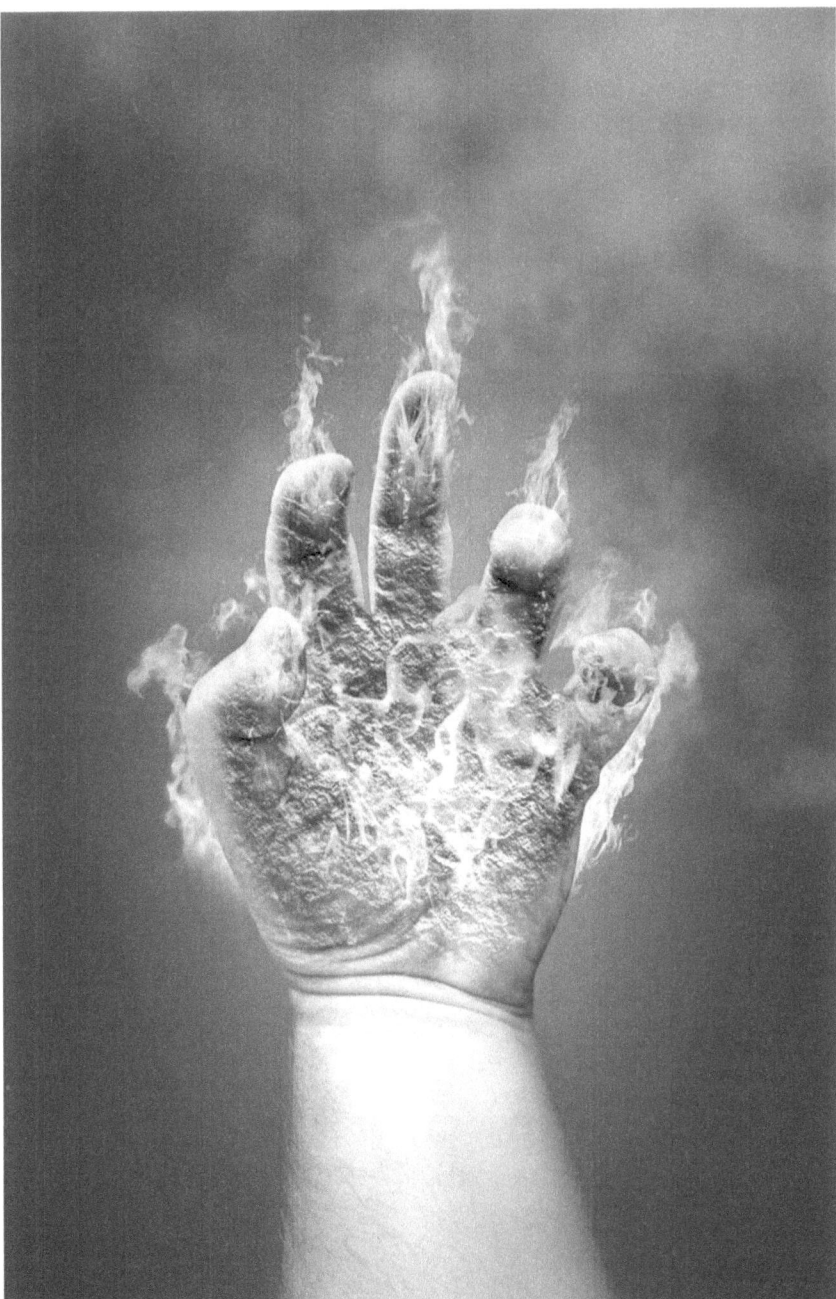

Figure 4.6 Hand aflame. Credit: Anonymous via Pixabay.

There's no daily life without storytelling; there are no hands, wrists, and fingers without storytelling; there's no medicine without storytelling; there's no healing without storytelling. Storytelling is as organic to us as breathing, circulation, digestion, locomotion, and all other aspects of biological living. Storytelling gives us understanding, meaning, memory, control, ownership.

We own our stories about our hands, and we own the experiences, sensations, and emotions of our hands. We're our *embodied narratives*. It's by changing our narratives that we change our hands, wrists, and fingers.

Skills and crafts

Simplifying and exaggerating my point, I'll say that slicing a tomato is a lofty undertaking bringing together hands, brains, farms, utensils, and recipes, not to mention the supply chain and the general unfolding of civilization over millennia.

A carpenter, a potter, a parent wrapping a baby in a blanket, a baker; a calligrapher, a bus driver, a person using sign language: a hundred skilled individuals are forever showing us how wonderful hands really are. Our job is to observe other people at work; sense and understand how they're using their hands; and retain, for our own purposes, something useful from their actions. Let's say you're a bass player. Watching a master craftsperson at work teaches you more about the double bass than taking a lesson from an impatient and incompetent bass teacher (Figures 4.7, 4.8, 4.9, and 4.10).

Figure 4.7 Hands of craft. Credit: Enric Sagarra.

THE POWER OF STORY

Figure 4.8 Looming hands. Credit: Nowaja.

Figure 4.9 Hand of sport. Credit: Pexels.

Figure 4.10 The archer. Credit: Kathe Busk.

Make a list, in your mind or on paper, of everything you do that engages your hands. Getting dressed, buttoning a shirt, tucking the shirt into the trousers, putting on socks, putting on shoes and tying them. As a little kid, you had to learn every one of these seemingly simple actions. And for some of these actions, you had to practice many dozens of times until you became comfortable with them. Making coffee, buttering a piece of toast, opening a jar of honey, spreading the honey on the buttered toast. These quotidian acts probably happen without you thinking too much about them, unless something goes wrong: for instance, when you can't open the jar of honey.

Here's a poem that you and I composed after spending a day watching our hands and playing with them.

Hands, Wrists, Fingers

Grab, grip, clutch, clasp, snatch;
Seize, clamp, hold, pinch, catch.

Press, push, slam, tap, pound;
Mold, shape, trace, weave, bound.

Flick, punch, squeeze, jab, smack;
Point, wave, snap, nod, crack.

Twist, turn, spin, switch, wring;
Toss, throw, hurl, drop, fling.

Pick, pull, tug, yank, slide;
Shift, swipe, stroke, rub, glide.

Sensuality

Sensoriality is your capacity to sense and to perceive things; sensuality is your capacity to enjoy sensations. Sometimes sensuality has an erotic connotation. We acknowledge and celebrate this dimension of sensuality, and we also extend our understanding of sensuality to encompass the sheer delight in receiving all types of pleasurable sensations: touching cashmere, silk, linen, satin; running hot water over our hands on a cold day; using our fingers to lick clean a bowl of cookie dough; squeezing a purring cat against our sternum and neck; falling in love with a partner because of his or her hands; shaking hands with someone we like and lingering on the handshake for the pleasure of it (Figure 4.11).

Here's an exercise. Use both hands to touch yourself from top to bottom, slowly and repeatedly. Your hands have cleansing and healing powers, real or imagined; by touching your hair, you make it grow; by touching the skin

Figure 4.11 Hands of clay. Credit: Pexels.

on your face, you make it glow. Have your fingers befriend your bony elbows, your hairy or non-hairy thighs, your nose, your belly button. How many square centimeters of skin do you have? Touch all the centimeters within your reach. How many layers of varying texture does your skin have? Let's speak Latin for a second: epidermis, dermis, hypodermis; voluptatis sensavorium pleasurabilis. Shower gel: your job is to find two or three brands of sweet-smelling shower gel and spend regular time in the sensavorium. Your hands, wrists, and fingers are the indispensable agents of your sensual explorations. You don't simply focus on your skin; you focus on your hands as they touch your skin. A good shower teaches your hands more than a distracted practice session at the music studio (Figure 4.12).

Musical instruments, too, have their bodies and their skins. For a moment, stop practicing and making music, and instead touch and stroke your instrument. Hold your flute or clarinet as you would a cat or a baby. Caress the flute with a light touch, perhaps with your eyes closed, and marvel at the variety of shapes: the tube, the head joint, the embouchure, the keys. This may be quite a revealing experience: the rush to practice and prepare for a performance may be lessening the sensitivity of your hands, wrists, and fingers to the instrument's characteristics, its personality, its sensoriality, its breathing soul, to coin an expression.

All instruments have sensuous potentialities. You know your flute well, but have you ever touched an ophicleide, a nyckelharpa, a bandoneon? At your next rehearsal, convince your friends and colleagues to trade instruments and engage in a collective soundless exploration of surfaces. Let your hands fall in love with a tuba, with a triangle, with a hurdy-gurdy. When your hands fall in love with an object, they're falling in love with their own selves, their own sensuous and sensorial qualities. "I love touching this object; it means that I love the sensations and emotions in my hands as I touch this object."

Figure 4.12 Hands of closeness. Credit: Rijksmuseum.

Part II
THE LANGUAGE OF THE HANDS

Figure II Speaking hands. Credit: Chu Viết Đôn.

Chapter 5

EXPRESSIVE GESTICULATION

Imagine a complete database of every conceivable gesture: all gestures for all purposes, from all cultures and all personality types. In your daily life and in your music making, you're an individual embodiment of this infinite database, occupying your own corner of it. Going deeper into the gestural database and expanding your territory is a sure way to enhance your Creative Health.

This chapter presents games and exercises that require make-believing and pretending. You might find it unnatural to practice gestures that don't reflect your personality or your aesthetics. But would you like to improve the use of your hands, wrists, and fingers? Would you like to refine your instrumental technique and energize your musical interpretations? Would you like to heal your hurts and overcome your handicaps? Come and play these games, even if they seem strange to you (Figure 5.1).

To start, you'll speak and gesticulate in a variety of styles. Use a paragraph of written text, a poem, a set of instructions; count numbers out loud, in sequence or at random; talk to an imaginary audience; or practice together with a friend, a colleague, or a student.

1. Use both hands together, working symmetrically as a sort of metronome or marker of emphasis. Always use the same gesture, maybe a chopping motion which could be big or small in amplitude. You'll embody a one-gesture personality.
2. Use a single hand, just adding a few random waves to the discourse. Do two versions, with your dominant and your nondominant hand. The waves are different from the chopping motions of the previous exercise (Figure 5.2).
3. Think the paragraph to yourself and gesticulate silently. It's not sign language, but an improvised choreography. We often do it when we're having conversations with imaginary people in our minds.
4. Waggle a finger at your audience, for instance the index finger of your dominant hand. The waggling finger has multiple meanings, some

Figure 5.1 Hands of gesticulation. Credit: Rijksmuseum.

friendly, some hostile. There are a lot of variables for you to play with: the amplitude and frequency of the gesture, the rhythm of the waggling, the shapes drawn by the arm as you waggle your finger.

5. Fists have expressed many emotions over the centuries, including powerful political messages. There are fists of celebration, fists of violent threats, fists of playfulness. Make two loose fists and tap one into the other, lightly. Or make a tight fist and bang on the table as you shout imprecations and certitudes.

Figure 5.2 Expressing joy. Credit: Rona Abdullah.

6. The arms, hands, wrists, and fingers can do all the gesticulation. Or the head, neck, and shoulders can get involved. Do a dance of gesticulation, starting from complete stillness and gradually adding small increments of bodily motion. Do you like homework? Play Ravel's "Bolero" in the background and sustain your steady crescendo of gesticulation over twenty minutes.
7. Make smooth slow gestures as if you were under water, pushing against the pleasant resistance of the warm sea. It's possible to talk at a fast clip and gesticulate at a slower tempo.
8. Become a rotational choreographer, turning your forearms and wrists. Good models for this style are Tai Chi practitioners and Hawaiian hula dancers.
9. Take on a priestly tone of voice, slow and caring, perhaps ponderous, perhaps ludicrous. And let your hands choreograph the message. Remember, you can do all these exercises in the abstract (counting numbers, for instance); reading paragraphs out loud (from a newspaper or from a sacred text); speaking nonsense; making sound effects; speaking normally; or in silence.
10. Allow yourself to channel a stereotypical or caricatural Mediterranean speaker, passionate and intense, with strongly accented gestures. Are you craaaazy? There are many cultures where vivid gesticulation is an integral part of communication. Individuals from the same culture might share a common vocabulary of gestures, but they also have unique personal styles. You, too, can express an individual style while practicing a shared vocabulary.
11. Become the professor at the lectern. Standing ramrod straight, bring fingertips of both hands together, then take them apart. The vessel formed by the 10 fingertips in contact can feel surprisingly integrative.
12. Become the hand caresser, intertwining your fingers and separating them, rubbing your palms, squeezing your hands gently.
13. Sit at a couch or armchair. Park one elbow on the armrest but allow the forearm and hand to move. Talk and gesticulate, without letting your elbow leave the armrest. You're training yourself to control degrees of movement. In this case, the fixed elbow invites the upper arm and upper body to stay relatively still, and the forearm, hand, wrist, and fingers to do the talking.
14. Sit at a table with both elbows on the table. Talk and gesticulate. This is the two-armed version of the previous exercise.
15. Become the person who never gesticulates. Rest your hands on your lap or on a table in front of you. Sit on your hands if you must. The absence of gesticulation doesn't come naturally to everyone.

Our Expressive Friends

Watch other people and see how they express themselves: family members, strangers out in the street, politicians making speeches, actors and actresses on screen. The shy, the extroverted, the clownish, the insistent; the liar, the snake oil salesman, the trickster, the shapeshifter; the dancerly, the painterly, the singerly; the Mediterranean, the Germanic, the Latin, the Japanese; the terribly self-conscious, the terribly self-ignorant; the affected, the charming, the annoying; the forgettable, the marvelous, the horrible. The number of gesticulating personalities is huge.

Imagine two people who speak without using hand gestures. One is comfortable with it, speaking with a melodious voice and charming smiles of many hues. The other is stiff, afraid to move, afraid to be seen and to be heard. The two people are more different from each other than they're alike.

Sometimes we respond strongly to a gesticulating style: "I can't stand watching this person talk." "Wow, she's so expressive! I love her!" I remember a college professor from 45 years ago. He stretched his hands wide and brought the fingers back, half twisting them. Oh, it was so stiff, so ugly, so awkward, so ... so something! And he did it practically nonstop! Yuck!

Sometimes we look at an old friend, and suddenly we capture something about her that had escaped our attention: "She is a rotational type, her hands always cupped in a convex shape, always, always." From another friend we notice that he often doesn't finish his sentences, and his hands offer a sort of compromise, talking for him when he can't find his words. Hands tending toward a grip or a vise; floppy hands; hands that seem to suffer from cold, every day of the year; elongated fingers that make us think of Byzantine art: a friend is talking to us, gesticulating in her normal way, and she doesn't realize that we're on a head trip to Byzantium, circa 1300 AD (Figure 5.3).

The task is to become keenly alert to the linguistic charge of everyone's hands. To notice, to observe, to appreciate, to understand the expressive hands; to find inspiration in elegant and eloquent hands, and to learn by negation when we see hands talk in a manner we find ugly and we don't want our own hands to be like that; to catalog the styles and personalities of talking hands; to practice the art, again and again, and to become a polyglot of hand dialects; to love the hands and to love their language (Figure 5.4).

The Power of a Single Gesture

Gestures depict the entire range of human emotion from hate to love, from the profane to the sacred. Gestures have so much power that cultures have developed obligations, taboos, and interdictions regarding gestures.

Figure 5.3 Hands of dialogue. Credit: Magdalena Maier.

Figure 5.4 Hands of conversation. Credit: Mircea Iancu.

The well-known gesture of giving the finger is considered phallic and goes back to ancient Greece and Rome. Its symbol is deeply imprinted in the minds of the multitudes. For some people, it's taboo to make the gesture. My late mother, for instance, never swore and never gave the finger; not even jokingly would she have been able to do it.

Some gestures are illegal—for instance, making the Nazi salute in Germany and Austria. You risk going to jail for raising your arm. If you minimize the power of symbols, it seems absurd and unjust to be punished for raising your arm. But if you accept the power of symbols, the raised arm is terrifying.

Our everyday "Okay" gesture of ringed thumb and index with other fingers extended manifests itself in Buddhism, in classical Greece, and in many other contexts. In my native Brazil, traditionally it was an extremely rude insult, although the Americanization of Brazilian culture has changed this to some degree. Back in the 1950s, when he was vice president, Richard Nixon visited Brazil. He emerged from his plane with both hands held high and displaying the Okay sign. He meant it as a positive message of friendship, a big extroverted "Hello!" from the big American cousin. The Brazilian people were deeply offended, because in Brazil—no, it's too rude; I can't tell you what the gesture meant to us back then.

Let's imagine that each gesture is a particular manifestation of an archetype called Gesture—the source of all possible gestures with all possible meanings. This source is terribly powerful: Gesture can lift you, and Gesture can squash you. "I acknowledge that gestures are powerful. Here's my flute. I have something to tell you, and my fingers are the absolute masters of meaningful, well-directed gestures that will lift you."

Mudras are symbolic hand gestures widely used in Buddhism, yoga, and Indian dance, among other contexts. In Buddhism, they're spiritual gestures that represent different states of consciousness. Sitting in the lotus position, Buddha touches the Earth with the right hand, palm facing inward, while the left rests on his lap. The gesture symbolizes enlightenment, calling the Earth to witness it. In Indian dance, highly stylized and codified gestures tell complex narratives, convey emotions, and illustrate themes and ideas. In yoga, different mudras channel different energies.

Each of these traditions requires devotion and practice. For our immediate purposes, we distill the essence of mudras by picking a few pertinent words: consciousness, narrative, emotion, energy. Now we condense these four words into a single one: intentionality (Figures 5.5 and 5.6).

We'll do a few improvisatory exercises employing our distilled intentionality.

Figure 5.5 Hands of deep thought. Credit: Minh Huỳnh.

Figure 5.6 Hand of dance. Credit: Shutterstock | Dmitry Rukhlenko.

1. Perform a gestural choreography in slow motion, using a sequence of gestures from your daily life or from the recesses of your imagination. Use each hand in turn, then both together. Make each gesture deliberately, and pass from gesture to gesture just as deliberately. Aim for continuity and coherence. Sing something to yourself, play music in the background, or perform in silence. It's up to you to consider this exercise a silly travesty of traditional Indian dance, or an interesting entry point toward coherent gesticulation.
2. Perform another gestural choreography, now following a simple predetermined pattern: make a loose fist; make the V for Victory gesture; go back to a loose fist; make the OK gesture. Put the sequence on a deliberate, slow, continuous, coherent loop. Remember that the same gesture may have different meanings in different cultures. Intentionality will carry the day.
3. Practice these gestures in isolation:
   a. Palms together, fingers pointing up (generally considered a prayerful gesture, also signaling gratitude).
   b. Okay (and we won't worry about the Brazilians).
   c. V for Victory (with the palm facing outward, otherwise it's an insult).
   d. Crossed fingers for luck (middle finger over index finger).
   e. "Live Long and Prosper" (the Vulcan greeting from "Star Trek," palm open, index and middle fingers together, ring and little fingers together).

Now practice a deliberate, slow choreography alternating the palms together (signaling gratitude) and the four other gestures. Repeat the sequence as many times as you wish:

Palms / okay, palms / victory, palms / luck, palms, Vulcan;
Palms / okay, palms / victory, palms / luck, palms, Vulcan;
Palms / okay, palms / victory, palms / luck, palms, Vulcan;
Palms / okay, palms / victory, palms / luck, palms, Vulcan…

The Grammelot

Perhaps you're familiar with "Pingu," a Claymation series produced by the Swiss (and later by the British) and featuring a family of anthropomorphic penguins. Short episodes using plasticine figurines feature Pingu, the main character, getting in and out of trouble and dealing with his family and friends. The episodes are clever and touching, and easy to find on YouTube.

For our purposes, the main thing is that all characters in all episodes are voiced by a single person: the Italian actor Carlo Bonomi (1937–2022), using a made-up language full of onomatopoeia, babbling, mumbling, and seemingly existing words that don't officially exist.

Technically, this sort of language is called *grammelot*. The language is a sort of parody, a joke in itself; amazingly, Bonomi created all lines of dialogue without a script. It's said that he drew inspiration from the *commedia dell'arte*, a style of street theater that arose in Italy in the 1500s and is based on stock characters, scripted routines, and a lot of improvisation. Characters from the *commedia dell'arte* include a greedy old man, a know-it-all doctor, the young couple in love, Arlequin (Harlequin), and others. The genre has left its mark, having for instance influenced Molière and Marivaux in their comic plays. Pulcinella, another stock character, eventually offered inspiration for Stravinsky when he composed his ballets "Petrushka" and also the eponymous "Pulcinella," in which Stravinsky soups up some Italian Baroque music. Characters also pop up in paintings, for instance in Picasso's multiple explorations of Arlequin.

In other words, it's likely that *commedia dell'arte* has long played some little role in your life, indirectly educating your aesthetics and your sense of theater and language (Figure 5.7).

Watch Pingu episodes online; they really are funny and clever. Hear Carlo Bonomi improvise a universal language that every child in the world understands, with no need for dubbing or subtitles. The language (in the varied voices of many characters, including Pingu, Pinga, and Pingi) contains all the information needed for us to follow the plot, sense the emotions of each character, and have our own emotions as we sympathize and empathize with the characters' struggles.

Your fancy homework, then, is to improvise a nonsense language (a grammelot) with musical and rhythmic plausibility, and to gesticulate while speaking it: a convincing made-up language with its own gestures, its rhetoric, its choreography. A successful performance of this special homework will carve interesting paths in your brain, establishing connections between brain functions that tend to work separately rather than together. Once these connections are established, your retrained brain can put its ease with language and gesture at the service of your music making.

Your grammelot, inspired by Pingu and his godfather Carlo Bonomi, is useful in other ways, too. You can use it to talk to yourself, to your students, to members of your string quartet. Suppose you want to explain an exercise to a student. If you explain it in English or in any other well-established language, your student may understand it or misunderstand it in various ways. Explaining it in grammelot, while performing the exercise at the same time,

Figure 5.7 Commedia dell'arte. Credit: Brita Seifert.

allows your student to understand it or misunderstand it in new and different ways. Depending on context and timing, your student might understand the grammelot version much more quickly than the English version.

Grammelot is a way to talk to your own self when something is bugging you and you don't even know what it is that is bugging you. It might be a message from the subconscious regarding a problem, a situation, a person;

Figure 5.8 Hands of explanation. Credit: WikimediaImage.

the message might be a reminder, an insight, a solution. Not knowing exactly what you're doing or why, you might start mumbling to yourself in grammelot and suddenly you receive the message. Mumbling in grammelot while gesticulating is particularly effective. It's the right brain's way of saying, "Let me think [...]" (Figure 5.8).

The Pencil

Take a pencil in your hand. Talk and gesticulate. Let the pencil be part of your discourse, as if you come from a village with a special dialect that absolutely requires the use of a pencil. The pencil can be a sixth finger, a wand, a ceremonial dagger used not to kill people but to cut through ignorance. Use your dominant hand and your nondominant hand; pass the pencil from hand to hand; hold the pencil with both hands while you talk. Use the pencil to point, to exhort, to admonish; use the pencil to hypnotize your listeners, or just to capture their attention and keep them engaged.

I often hold a pencil while talking to students online. I don't know how to explain it, but the pencil seems to organize my hands, to structure them; the pencil gives me a little reassurance; my inner child says, "I have something," which is different from "I have nothing." The pencil is an extra finger, long and bony, well designed and elegant. The finger-like pencil can write and draw, but it can also poke and perforate. The pencil is a laser pointer in my imagination.

The pencil represents, for now, the instrument that you'll hold soon and that you'll play with the same clarity of intention. You'll hypnotize your listeners with the clarinet and the French horn; you'll persuade your listeners to go on a trip with you; you'll elevate their perception of the world, including their perception of their own selves in the world. It's a big deal. And to become the orator and the oracle addressing the crowd, it's valid to practice multiple intermediate steps. The pencil is a scepter, an oboe, a duduk, your violin bow, your conducting baton.

Coincidence

For this exercise you need to snap your fingers, preferably with the right hand. If you aren't comfortable snapping, clap instead. Or tap a surface. Or tap the floor with a foot. The main point is for you to make some sort of sound with some body part (other than your mouth, which will be busy speaking or singing).

1. Say something, anything; read a paragraph out loud; declaim a poem you know; say a single sentence many times on a loop; count out loud, from one onward in a linear progression (one, two, three …). While talking, snap your fingers so that the snap happens at the exact same time as an emphasized syllable in what you're saying:

    "Good morning, my dear friends."
    "Good MOR-ning, my dear friends."
    "Good morning, my DEAR friends."
    "Good MOR-ning, my DEAR, dear friends."

    Aim for an absolute coincidence of syllable and snap: no hesitation, no calculation; a precise event in time and space, right here, right *now*: "Good MOR-ning!"
2. Once you get the hang of it, go to your instrument. Speak as before and tap a note at the piano or the cello to coincide with an emphasized syllable. Speak while holding your flute in playing position and articulate a note with fingers of one or both hands.
3. Still at the instrument, play a melody using the finger motions that you normally employ in playing the melody, but speak the melody instead of playing it. Every syllable of your speech (emphasized or not) will coincide with a note that you articulate with one or more fingers.

4. Now play an actual melody, composition, or improvisation, and keep speaking it in your mind as you play. The linguistic impulse is firmly established, and the playing becomes coherent and expressive.

Containment and Latency

Imagine two extremes: people who never use their hands as a complement to speech, and people who always use their hands when they talk. The two extremes are "never" and "always," which are extremes of frequency. And now imagine two new extremes: people who make discreet little gestures when they speak, and people who gesticulate with their entire bodies when they speak—a contrast between the invisible and the visible, the subtle and the exaggerated, the introverted and the extroverted. The two extremes are "a little" or "a lot," which are extremes of amplitude.

Few people dwell in the extremes. Most of us are somewhere in between, varying our frequency and amplitude according to circumstance. We adopt different gestural vocabularies when watching a sports event with our friends and when asking our banker for a loan.

Creative Health invites you to have a diverse vocabulary that you access with skill and freedom. The infinite database contains your gestures, in both senses of the word: it gathers your thousand latent gestures in a convenient place, and it keeps the gestures from spilling out when you prefer to keep them in. When they work together, latency and containment are your two best friends (Figure 5.9).

Figure 5.9 Hands of peace. Credit: senjakelabu29.

Chapter 6

SOUNDS MADE AND SOUNDS HEARD

A thing often isn't what you think it is about. Clapping isn't about clapping.

Clapping seems like an ordinary action that you perform without thinking. And yet, behind the ordinary action lies a world of possibilities. All you need is to pay attention. It changes everything.

Let's list a few of the reasons for which we clap and the energies we employ to clap: polite applause; extroverted celebration in a group; a reaction of surprise and delight at something that happened suddenly and unexpectedly, a soccer goal, for instance, a clever movement by a street dancer, a joke; forced clapping, when the unwilling assembly must clap to honor the dictator. Proud clapping, celebratory clapping, encouraging clapping; hypocritical clapping, ironic clapping, sarcastic clapping; two hands coming together and making sounds to hurt someone or to annoy someone; clapping to insult, to protest, to dismiss.

Each reason to clap creates its own clapping techniques. Joy and anger don't clap alike. The virtuoso clapper taps into a hundred motivations, employs a hundred gestures, and produces a hundred different sounds. The hands of the virtuoso are clever, skillful, and adaptable. Clapping, then, can become another way for you to develop your Creative Health.

We'll write the clapping manual together, page by page, exercise by exercise.

1. Start not by clapping, but by choreographing a silent, fluid, slow dance of rotations. Engage the upper arms, elbows, forearms, wrists, hands, palms, and fingers, without letting the hands touch each other.
2. Now bring your hands together and caress them. Caressing is its own art, palm to palm, soft fingers intertwining soft fingers, gentle squeezing, gentle rubbing. The neuroscientist will tell you that caressing your hands changes your brain waves and gets your brain to release sweet chemicals. The acupuncturist will tell you that caressing your hands stimulates various meridians and provokes changes in the energy of the whole body and mind. The psychologist, the artist, the glovemaker, the lover will tell you many other things about caressing your hands.

3. Rubbing your palms together is also its own art. You might do it to warm your hands, to express satisfaction or anticipation. It's possible to threaten someone by simply rubbing your palms slowly while looking at your prey: "I'm going to take care of business." How much can you vary the rubbing? Fast, slow; soft hands, firm hands; flat hands, cupped hands.
4. Out of the caress, out of the rubbing palms, give birth to a soft clap, barely audible, barely visible. Let's call this a *newborn clap*, more potentiality than physicality, a faint sketch of a clap, an abstracted clap. Remember that the virtuoso clapper has many techniques and sounds in reserve, including the newborn clap.
5. Rubbing and caressing, initiating soft claps, start the study of variables and parameters: the overall shape of the hands, how curved or flat; the strength of the rubbing, very soft or a bit firmer now. Your newborn clap will grow little by little, gaining strength and power, loudness and resonance (Figures 6.1, 6.2, 6.3, and 6.4).
6. Dominant hand hitting the nondominant one, or vice versa; both hands coming together at the exact same time. Clap, and keep your hands glued together for a few seconds; clap, and immediately separate your hands. How far apart will you move your hands? If you like homework, practice a series of claps where you increase the distance between the hands by a few millimeters in between claps. There may be a hundred or more gradations of distance.
7. Can you change the distance between the hands but keep the volume of the clapping steady? Can you change the speed of your clapping but keep the volume steady? These are fine psychomotor skills that will make you a more intelligent and sensitive instrumentalist.
8. What is the motor of the clapping motion? It can be the full arm, the forearm only, the wrist only, or the fingers only. Cupped hands and flat hands don't make the same type of sound. Hands facing each other squarely and hands meeting at an angle don't make the same type of sound. Keep one hand steady as it receives the taps of the other hand. Tap with fingertips, with whole fingers, or with your palm; tap anywhere on the receiving hand. Tap the back of the hand.
9. Mixing and matching the variables allows you to make dozens of different sounds. Perform a *crescendo poco a poco*, keeping the beat steady. Now practice a *diminuendo poco a poco*, also keeping the beat steady. Then an *accelerando poco a poco*, keeping the volume steady; and, finally, a *ritardando poco a poco*, keeping the volume steady. It's more challenging that you think.

Figure 6.1 Youthful clapping. Credit: dhanelle.

Figure 6.2 Serious clapping. Credit: YasDO.

Figure 6.3 Sports clapping. Credit: Anonymous via Pixabay.

Figure 6.4 Clapping of encouragement. Credit: stefanopanizzo.

Figure 6.5 Traditional clapping. Credit: Jacqueline Macou.

10. Clap a famous tune from the classical music repertoire or from any other source. Many listeners will recognize "Happy Birthday" from its clapped rhythms alone. Improvise or compose a musical sequence of claps. Pick a time signature and clap varied rhythms within the time signature. Turn the metronome on and clap a duet with the metronome. Attempt two beats against three, three beats against four, syncopations, offbeats, hemiolas.
11. Flamenco is only one of the many musical styles in which clapping plays a defining, structural role. In flamenco, clapping is known as *palmas*, of which there are two main types: *palmas sordas* (muted claps) and *palmas claras* (clear claps). The complexity of rhythms in flamenco is remarkable. Watch flamenco performance clips and join in as a beginner student, clapping to the best of your ability.
12. Creative Health welcomes learning processes that include imitation, make-believe, bumbling along, and making indirect or intermittent progress. It also welcomes play for the sake of play, without obligatory progress (Figures 6.5 and 6.6).

Listen, Don't Listen

We often use our hands as an informal megaphone to amplify our voices. Let's become megaphone designers, shaping and reshaping our hands to see how they affect the volume and resonance of our voices.

Figure 6.6 Crowd clapping. Credit: Gigxels.

Get the left brain to help you with the variables you can play with: the shape of the hands, their firmness or softness, their placement around your mouth, their directionality. Test the one-hand megaphone in two models: dominant and nondominant hand. Cup one hand and place it next to your mouth. Speak, shout, sing, whisper, whistle. While using your voice, remove the cupped hand and speak or sing normally. Then bring the cupped hand back to its place. You'll become alert to the effect of the hand upon the voice, as well as upon your listening. Cup one hand next to the mouth; cup your other hand next to the ear; point the two cupping hands slightly toward each other; now speak or sing. I bet you'll be startled by the loudness and resonance of your voice.

Now use your hands, separately and together, to muffle or stifle your voice. The hand becomes a damper or sourdine, with its own dynamic range. Use the hand as a trumpet player would use a mute, alternately covering and uncovering your mouth and creating a sort of wah-wah effect. With a hand covering your mouth but not forcing it shut, speak or sing. It's possible that you'll be suddenly alert to the vibrations that your voice creates around your teeth and in your jaw. The hand has become your partner in the creation and perception of vibration.

An acoustic shell pavilion is a curved, arched, or angled structure like an outdoor amphitheater, its construction designed to organize sound, augment it, and propagate it more efficiently. To improve the reception of sound, we often bring our cupped hands singly or together to our ears. Then we become informal pavilion architects. Like with so many other habits of our daily lives, we can take the ordinary gesture and practice it consciously, not only to help us hear conversations in noisy restaurants but also to help us improve our psychomotor skills, our use of the hands, wrists, and fingers, our Creative Health.

Bring your hands to your ears. Aren't those appendages strange and wonderful? Delicately test the elastic cartilage of the outer ears, flicking them with your fingers. Drag fingertips lightly all around the ears' nooks and crannies. To make a study of your ears with your fingers is to give new and varied information to the fingers themselves. When your fingers do any one thing that's new and different, they gain in knowledge; when they do any one thing better than before, they gain in skill. It doesn't matter if the activity that renders the fingers knowledgeable and skillful is silly.

Cover an ear with a hand, flat or cupped. Your perception of sound and your perception of your own self are immediately altered. Cover both ears. Alternate covering and uncovering the ears. Tap your ears gently with your cupped hands, and you'll hear an intimate percussion recital.

SOUNDS MADE AND SOUNDS HEARD 93

When we want to hear better, we tend to cup our hands around the ears with the palms facing forward. But what if you want to hear something that's happening behind your back? Cup your hands, with the palms facing backward. Ask a friend to stand behind you and talk or whisper. You'll be amazed (Figures 6.7, 6.8, 6.9, 6.10, and 6.11).

The Hands as a Musical Instrument

You can use your hands as an ocarina, clasping the palms into a sort of medium-sized mango and blowing through a space between the thumbs.

You can use your hands to alter the sounds of your voice. Here's just an example: wrap your fingers around and in front of your nose, with the thumbs wrapped around your jaw. Talk and sing, and you won't recognize your voice.

The French psychologist Pierre Janet (1859–1947) coined a useful expression: *abaissement du niveau mental*, which means a lowering of the mental level, or a temporary decline in cognitive capabilities. He used it to refer to the mind under stress or trauma, when you might lose your intellectual acuity and find yourself disoriented, blocked, or paralyzed. Carl Jung (1875–1961) saw something potentially positive in the concept: when your reasoning loses its balance, deeply held contents from the unconscious might benefit from

Figure 6.7 Big ears. Credit: Holger Kraft.

Figure 6.8 Megaphone hands. Credit: Luisella Planeta LOVE PEACE.

Figure 6.9 Megaphone man. Credit: Harald Funken.

Figure 6.10 Noisy bird. Credit: ivabalk.

Figure 6.11 Hands of aural protection. Credit: Shutterstock | Studio Grand Web.

the incapacitated reason and rise to the surface. Depending on the circumstances, these contents might bring insight and healing. Jung suggested that you can use it as an actual technique and lower your mental level on purpose. Improvisational theater depends on this tool, because if you really, really think about what the improvisations entail, you really, really won't make a fool of yourself in front of people.

You can use one or both of your hands as an elastic vessel into which you blow a raspberry, shaping and reshaping the raspberry to make it particularly sonorous. (You know the raspberry: essentially, it's the sound of passing gas.) Imagine that blowing a raspberry is an art form. By varying the shape of your hands and the work of your cheeks, lips, and tongue, you can develop a wicked palette of sounds.

Figure 6.12 Silliness. Credit: Michael Kopp.

Creative Health welcomes a temporary decline in taste and judgment, within safe limits. Blow a raspberry; practice the art of blowing a raspberry into your hands; make your hands clever in their stupidity. Then sober up and take your clever and stupid hands to the piano, the cello, or any other musical activity. A façade of humor often hides a depth of skill (Figure 6.12).

Chapter 7

THE DANCE

In your mind's eye, picture an instrumentalist playing a solo. Let's say a pianist performing a prelude and fugue from Bach's "Well-Tempered Clavier." Now abstract the instrument—in your imagination, make the instrument invisible. Watch the pianist's hands air-play every note, every chord, and every sequence. In the absence of the piano, we can really see that the pianist's fingers are dancing an elaborate and meaningful choreography.

In truth, we don't need to make the instrument invisible. The dance of the fingers is obvious to the attentive eyes. Our job is to develop a skillful dancerly sensitivity in everything that we do with our fingers.

Find a surface: table, countertop, armrest, the back of a guitar, the sides of a cello. You'll be an amateur anatomist without a specialized vocabulary. And you'll be an amateur clown and mime delighting in doing fun and funny things, some of which will be ridiculous before they become divine.

We're used to finding parallels in the anatomy of the arms and legs: the upper arm is the thigh, the elbow is the knee, the forearm is the calf, the wrist is the ankle, the hand is the foot, the finger is the toe. I suggest that you tweak the imagery when you practice your finger dancing: the finger becomes not the reflection of a toe but of the whole leg and foot. You might think of the finger's three phalanges as the thigh, the lower leg, and the foot. This empowers the finger, giving it presence, strength, and agency.

The hand is in a state of readiness, all five fingers gently cupped and touching the table. To begin with, walk the index and middle fingers of your dominant hand on your chosen surface. Walk forward and backward. Let the index lead and the middle finger follow. Then trade roles: the middle finger leads, the index follows. There are many variables for you to play with: amplitude, speed, direction. Exercise your nondominant hand. Have both hands work together. Get your fingers to stand still, then ask the fingers to show you where their joints are and how they can flex them. Like dancers stretching and showing off, your fingers bend, curl, point, caress, drag, jump, run, and do pirouettes.

Do your exercise to a recorded soundtrack. It hardly matters what you play in the background: a minuet, a pop song, a march. But for the sake of explaining the exercise, let's say you'll play a recording of the first movement of Mozart's Symphony No. 40 in G minor, K. 555: something familiar, something with a steady and nervy beat, something interesting and beautiful, something that gets your fingers going. A quick visit to YouTube tells me that eight minutes is a plausible length for a performance of the movement. It may sound like a lot of time for a simple finger exercise, but the exercise is enriching and enjoyable.

The time signature is cut time: two half notes (or minims) per bar. The tempo indication is Molto allegro. Your choreography doesn't have to take the musical text literally. You can choreograph in opposition to the text: a fast passage danced slowly, for instance, or vice versa. Your fingers may walk and run, hop, pivot. Single fingers may perform solos. Command multiple fingers to dance a *pas de deux,* a *pas de trois,* a *pas de quatre.* Employ all styles of locomotion: walking, crawling, jumping, skipping, sliding, skating, marching, and moonwalking (Figures 7.1 and 7.2).

In joy and in pleasure, you're now a dancer at work. You occupy the stage as you respond to a musical masterpiece, making quick interpretative and technical decisions, practicing and playing. Watching your fingers dance is hypnotic. Your brain enters a slightly altered state, and you hallucinate: the fingers cease being extremities or peripheral body parts and become complete beings in themselves; the fingers become people; the fingers do what they want to do, not what you want them to do for you. Different fingers show different personalities, likes and dislikes, strengths and weaknesses, habits, tics. One finger will be an athletic dancer, a prima donna; another will be dainty and deft. Perhaps one of your fingers is hesitant and awkward, calling for tender loving care.

The Internet offers an infinite database of audio and video clips. Pick a dance clip: musical theater, ballet, old movies, new movies, breakdance. Watch it and let your fingers dance to what they see and hear.

You're familiar with lip-syncing, and perhaps you practice it without knowing it—for instance, when you listen to a song that you're familiar with. You can also practice finger-syncing. Sit at a table with your laptop. Watch a video clip of a pianist playing a piece. On the tabletop, finger-sync the piece. You're a little kid making up stuff, and your finger-syncing doesn't have to be accurate. The job isn't to finger-sync a virtuoso piece to perfection, but to respond creatively to a creative stimulus.

Young children learn by imitation, approximation, and intuition. Imagine a two-year-old growing up in a family of flamenco dancers. Imitating the family members, the child dances an abstract flamenco, approximating

Figure 7.1 Walking finger. Credit: Shutterstock | Montira Areepongthum.

Figure 7.2 Dancers. Credit: Evgen Rom.

the actual moves of the adults and professionals in the house. The little-kid approximation is necessary as an intermediate step toward adult mastery. But I think that the little-kid approximation is its own art form, with its own elegance and beauty, sometimes surpassing the beauty of the adult techniques. When you finger-sync, let the kid dance; let the kid make up stuff; let the made-up stuff be divine or ridiculous.

The Dance of the Wrists

The dance of the wrists will make you more comfortable with your own wrists, more alert to their existence, more grateful for all that they can do. Before the dance, do a warm-up routine. One hand massages the wrist of the other hand, squeezes it a little, pinches it a little, senses its construction under the skin, its nooks and crannies. Hair, skin, flesh, bones, like a layer cake. Now one hand wraps itself around the other wrist, feeling its size and shape, its thickness. What happens to a hand when you squeeze its wrist gently? It moves, it wants to move; it responds, it wants to respond. The hand is alive and lively. Your hands love your wrists, and the wrists love them back. Flex the wrists forward and backward. Turn the wrists sideways. Gently hold a forearm in place, and wave hello and bye-bye using the wrist only.

The word "wrist" comes from a Germanic root meaning "instep, back of the hand," derived from a Proto-Indo-European root meaning "to turn, to bend." Bend your wrists for the pleasure of bending them. Bend your wrists and lay your palms flat against a surface, vertical or horizontal. Bend your wrists as you wrap your arms around the arms of your friend or lover.

You're ready to dance. Start informally, moving your arms smoothly up in the air and in front of your chest, giving a silent speech in slow motion. Gesticulate expressively, as if you have something to say but you don't know exactly what. There's a lot of merit in a seemingly aimless improvisation. It removes the obligation of precision and meaning, an obligation that sometimes makes people stiff, careful, shy, afraid, hesitant, or discouraged. The misdirected search for precision risks making you imprecise.

Dance slowly, as if moving underwater, with fluid motions of your arms reminiscent of a lazy octopus having a good time for the sake of having a good time. Then the lazy octopus pretends to dance a strange flamenco, rotating the arms and wrists together, or rotating the wrists alone (Figures 7.3, 7.4, 7.5, and 7.6).

Figure 7.3 Flexed wrists. Credit: Myriams-Fotos.

Figure 7.4 Arms and flexed wrists. Credit: Ronald Plett.

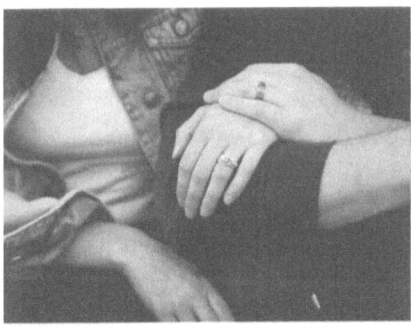

Figure 7.5 Intertwining. Credit: Pexels.

Figure 7.6 Flexed wrist and texture. Credit: Mabel Amber.

In Praise of the Imagination

We've all had transformative meetings with people: those close to us, those in the schools we've attended, those out in the world. We've passed through transformative events and situations, some tragic, some happy. We've had transformative travels. Seemingly small events also leave their mark. You hear a child laugh, and her happiness makes you feel good. The laugh is infectious, so you catch it. You can catch it from a real child who's right in front of you, or from watching a three-second video clip of a child who lives in a foreign land far away.

You read a novel, and you're so touched by it that you need to work through your own feelings. My sister-in-law cried for two days after reading Thomas Hardy's novel *Jude the Obscure*, which among other things deals with terribly unjust social mores. I was so upset after reading the novel *El Astillero* by Juan Carlos Onetti that I had to go talk to a therapist friend. (Onetti was a great

Uruguayan writer who mastered the art of depicting defeat, loneliness, and hopelessness.)

Works of fiction enter our psyches and disturb us, thanks to characters that only exist in the imaginations of the writers and their readers. Books, films, plays, works of art, TV shows, and a thousand other fruits of the human imagination speak to our own imaginations. We care for fictional characters; we're afraid of bad things happening to our favorite characters, and we get extremely aggressive, in our hearts, about paper villains. We identify with characters, including some that appear to have no similarities to our lived selves, our ordinary me-here-now; the fictional character can be of a different gender, different age, different nationality, different era, but we still see ourselves in the character, and the character in ourselves. And we care deeply about him or her.

What happens when you watch a great musical performance? You feel elevated, inspired, energized; gratitude and wonderment flow through your veins; after the concert you go home transformed, and for some hours or days (and sometimes longer) you practice your own instrument with more clarity, more discipline, more creativity. It doesn't matter if you're an oboist and the performance you attended was by a violinist: the positive effects propagate regardless of the specifics involved. Watching an inspired pianist can make you a better cellist; watching an inspired game of table tennis can make you a better cellist; watching an inspiring horse run an obstacle course can make you a better cellist.

Life consists of a sequence of translations. One of my siblings says something, and unconsciously I translate it into a language suited to my habits of understanding, my filters, my preferences. I look at a score, and I translate it into sounds, fingerings, bowings, articulations, tempi. No other musician, now or ever, will make the exact same translation of this same score.

Translation and imagination work together, and—if we think about it—they never stop working. You're reading this paragraph and translating it into your ways of understanding, thereby agreeing or disagreeing with the paragraph's arguments. And your imagination is forming impressions, perhaps visual or aural, triggered by the paragraph. If you put the book down, your translation and imagination will quickly and smoothly turn to another set of triggers—maybe your piano, maybe a household task, maybe a child who might be near you or at school several blocks away.

A single photo can trigger memories, inner narratives, emotions, physical sensations. This is true of a framed photo of your late mother and of a snapshot of a hurt child featured in a newspaper article about a car crash. And the triggered sensations run the gamut of the senses. You hear the child's pain, you sense it in your flesh and bones, you smell the burned tires of the car turned upside down. Your reaction is embodied.

"A lazy octopus, dancing a slow flamenco under water." Your translation and your imagination start working, and your reaction to these inner processes is embodied. I'm inviting you to embrace the process and facilitate it, simply by your willingness to play the game. I think you already play the game, possibly without being completely aware of it. I know it seems silly, but saying "yes" to something that you're already doing can make the thing more present, more lived, more urgent.

The imagination is the source of what we do, see, feel, think, believe, and respond to. The cat that you caress has its material and physical existence; objectively, it exists as a cat. But your mind, heart, and hands are having a subjective experience caressing and squeezing the cat. The cat becomes story, narrative, symbol; the cat becomes meaning, intention, commitment; the cat becomes friend, companion, witness; the cat becomes Cat. Someone else squeezing the very same cat will be squeezing a different cat because his or her imagination perceives the cat differently from you.

An octopus that we see in an aquarium, one that we play with while scuba diving, one that we watch on the Internet: any octopus will trigger stories and emotions in our imagination. Stretching the idea just a little, we'll say that every octopus is imaginary. Our imaginary octopus is multitentacled, elastic, adaptable; a good swimmer, a good player; able to grasp things and to let go of things; able to play hide-and-seek, to appear and to disappear; curious,

Figure 7.7 Flamenco. Credit: Iatya Prunkova.

Figure 7.8 Octopus. Credit: Erik Tanghe.

inventive, intelligent, creative. By a sort of projective osmosis, when we watch the octopus or when we imagine it, we absorb some of its qualities. We want to be like the octopus, and we do become a little bit more like the octopus because the imagination is the most powerful force in the world.

"A lazy octopus, dancing a slow flamenco under water." "Yes! Those are my wrists!" And an image, a joke, a stretch of the imagination, an absurdity is now helping you develop healthy and adaptable hands, wrists, and fingers (Figures 7.7 and 7.8).

Part III
SENSITIVITY AND CREATIVITY

Figure III Capable hands. Credit: Keith Johnston.

Chapter 8

TEXTURES

Let's imagine a school devoted exclusively to the exploration of textures. Tradition says that the school is in the foothills of the Himalayas. Students learn how to recognize specific materials, how to tell fine sandpaper from rough sandpaper, how to gauge resistance in spring mechanisms, how to read Braille, and how to tell a 3B pencil from a 4B pencil simply by touching the pencil to paper. Over the years, students become alert and sensitive, and their textural skills end up influencing their entire lives.

In truth, this is how every life unfolds: as an endless series of encounters with textures and gradations. Your kitchen is a textural school. Peeling a carrot is different from peeling a potato; their textures aren't exactly alike. Placing a knife against a tomato, you sense the tomato's texture and its degree of resistance, and you make quick psychomotor decisions as to the angle of the blade on the tomato and the force you'll apply to slice it. Dinner is a series of textural assessments (Figure 8.1).

Walk barefoot through your house, and your feet will marvel at how many different textures the floors offer you: rugs thick and thin, stones rough and smooth, planks and slats, tiles, each texture with its own personality and its own physicality. There's no confusing stone and rug; there's no confusing wool and wood. Your feet are lovers of texture, and so are your hands.

Our imaginary school of textures takes on students of all ages and all levels of talent and experience, ranging from a complete beginner to a complete master. The awkward beginner will trip over a rug because insensitive feet didn't capture the rug's texture and placement on the slippery floor. The beginner will peel an unripe mango only to regret the waste of a potentially delicious fruit. The beginner will use a 2B pencil to do a sketch, not having sensed that a 6B pencil would work better for the task at hand. The beginner will play a few notes on the school's piano and will quickly decide that the piano is bad, difficult to play, impossible to play, useless; I hate it. And the master will come around, caress the piano keys, sense the relationship between the keys and the rest of the instrument, play those same few notes, and make the piano purr and sing. The world doesn't have any bad pianos

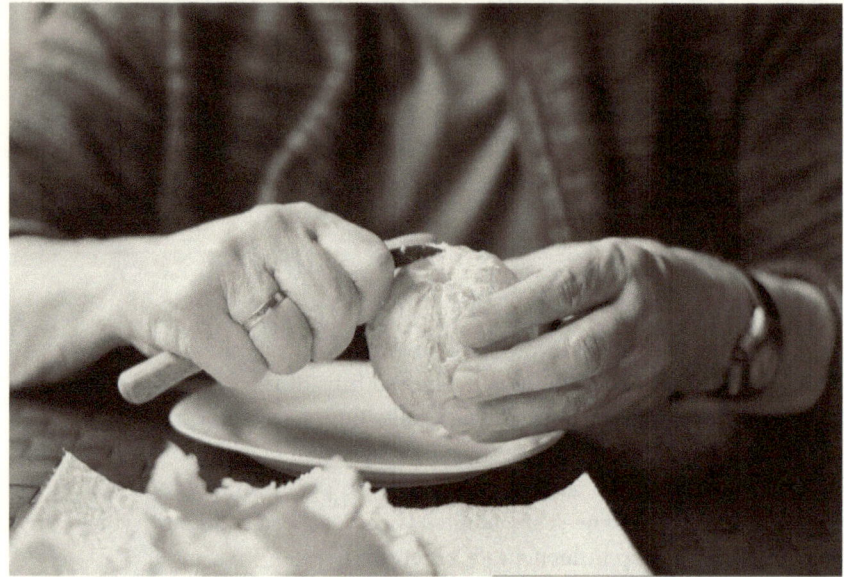

Figure 8.1 Peeling hands. Credit: congerdesign.

in it, but it does have pianos with wildly differing personalities. Personality is texture, and texture is personality. Touch your lover's skin, and you'll subjectively capture your lover's personality. And your lover may be your harp, your guitar, your viola.

Your job is to progress steadily as a student of textures. Consider it a full-time occupation.

Textiles

Your existence is made of ceaseless encounters with textiles: silk, cotton, linen, polyester, wool, cashmere; blankets, curtains, kitchen towels; socks, shirts, trousers, sweaters, coats. Let's suppose that you're the type of person who gets dressed in a hurry, and that's it for your perception of textiles. Your job is to slow down, to separate the exploration of textiles from the rushed daily chore, to linger over a shirt or sweater, to turn the textile into a sort of cat or lover whom you caress happily.

Here are three ways of practicing.

1. Let your daily life be your school of textile textures, and enjoy your textiles every day, all day long.
2. If 24/7 is too much commitment, punctuate your day with periods of a few minutes when you touch, handle, and caress the textiles in your home.

3. Set a time to concentrate on textiles. Gather as many textiles as practicable. Lay your textiles on a table or sit with them on a couch or armchair. Pick a textile at random and explore it in detail, touching it lightly and firmly, wrapping it around your hands and fingers, rubbing it against your face. Closing your eyes might change your perception of the object and of your own hands. Pick another textile and repeat the procedure, touching, handling, wrapping, rubbing. Now pass between textiles, noticing their differences and, to the extent you can, noticing these differences as quickly as possible. Within a single textile, there may be many textures: the ribs on a sweater sleeve, the little labels sewn inside the sweater, a logo, stitches. Sensing the textile is synonymous with sensing your hands. You're forever working on the perception of your perception, as it were. Textile, hands, perception; cat, lover, scarf: the scarf starts talking to you, it starts making love to your hands. "I'll never forget the day I felt cashmere for the first time." "I'll never forget the day when I played the flute and I really sensed the springs under my finger pads."

Becoming sensitive to textiles and their textures makes your hands smarter. And with those smarter hands, you can approach any musical goal. Let's take the cello as an example. The normal concert cello has four strings, tuned (from the bottom up) C G D A. There exist five-string cellos and cellos tuned to other combinations of pitches. But for the purposes of our discussion, we'll stick with the normal concert cello.

The strings have different thicknesses; the lower the string, the thicker it is. You, the imaginary cellist playing our imaginary cello, will touch the C string lightly, then the G string, the D, the A; you'll immediately sense their individual thicknesses, and you'll become able to tell them apart without looking at them, through touch alone. And you won't need to touch the strings repeatedly before knowing which string is the C, which the G: one touch, and the information will be clear to you (Figures 8.2, 8.3, and 8.4).

Cello strings run from the pegbox to the cello's tail, resting on a nut just below the pegbox, hovering above the fingerboard, resting again on the bridge, and then being held by the tailpiece. If you pluck a string at its midpoint, you'll sense a certain degree of resistance; if you pluck it near the bridge, you'll sense a greater degree of resistance. Much as you can tell the difference between cotton and linen, you'll be able to sense gradations of resistance up and down the string—and you'll be able to mix and match, for instance, knowing whether a string is the A or the D and whether you're touching it at the midpoint or near the bridge. And the gradations of resistance will invite gradations of pressure from your playing hands.

Figure 8.2 Texture of fibers. Credit: wal_172619.

Figure 8.3 Texture of textile. Credit: Gundula Vogel.

Figure 8.4 Texture of fabric. Credit: hartono subagio.

The cello is only an illustration. Every musical instrument offers a wealth of textural information: the piano and the guitar, the harp, the flute; it doesn't matter. Suppose you have a tambourine in the house. Your cotton, linen, and silk sensitivity allows you to sense fine gradations of resistance on the surface of the tambourine's membrane. And thanks to that sensitivity, you can hit each point on the membrane with a different touch, producing many types of sounds. Texture sensitivity helps you find the sweet spot (Figures 8.5 and 8.6).

Papers

Papers are like textiles: they're essential to your life, they have wonderful textures for you to explore, and they can help your hands, wrists, and fingers become more sensitive and adaptable.

Catalog the types of paper currently in your home: newspaper, glossy magazine, tissue paper, wrapping paper, office paper, envelope, cardboard, paper towel, Kraft paper, Post-It, toilet paper, postcard. The list isn't exhaustive.

What qualities do different papers have? They may be smooth, grainy, rough, fine; matte, glossy, satin; opaque, translucent, transparent; absorbent or nonabsorbent; coated, textured, embossed. Each of these qualities welcomes your touch, and your touch is interested in each of these qualities.

Figure 8.5 Hand sensing layers. Credit: Rijksmuseum.

For some people, paper is just paper. For others, paper is a marvel of human ingenuity, a marvel of textures, a marvel of uses, a marvel. Hands, wrists, and fingers of indifference work in a certain way; hands, wrists, and fingers of appreciation work in another way; hands, wrists, and fingers of adoration are themselves worthy of adoration.

Figure 8.6 Hands sensing an instrument. Credit: Rijksmuseum.

Would you write and send a note of condolences on a Post-It? No, never, what a question! Different papers for different purposes; different textures for different purposes. We assign value to paper, including bureaucratic value, artistic value, ceremonial and religious value. We frame diplomas and display them proudly. Your birth certificate, which is "just a piece of paper," is symbolic of your existence on this Earth. If you doubt me, order a copy of your birth certificate for the purpose of tearing it to shreds or setting fire to it or flushing it down the toilet. You recoil at the idea, don't you?

I think it's useful to consider that all types of paper are the beloved children of Paper, a deity with infinite imagination. The papyri of Egypt, using the pith of the *papyrus* plant, and the parchments of Greece and Rome, using animal skins, were the sacred first imaginings of Paper. Two thousand years ago, the deity compelled the Chinese to create paper using mulberry bark and hemp. Later, the deity thought of making paper out of wood pulp, and paper became cheaper and accessible, revolutionizing the world. More recently, the deity has taken to inventing electronic paper. It's too soon to know if this is a good or bad thing, but your hands, wrists, and fingers probably have an opinion about it already. And if not an opinion, certainly a feeling.

As with the textiles, you have three good choices: let your daily life be your school of paper textures; punctuate your days with moments where you explore paper; or set aside chunks of time where you train your hands, wrists, and fingers to become paper experts. Thanks to the possibility of information transfer, the hands that become more sensitive to paper become more sensitive in themselves, as it were—to the benefit of your music making (Figure 8.7).

Figure 8.7 Papers. Credit: Sergii Koviarov.

Sponge, Towel, Book

Gather the following objects: a kitchen towel; a sponge, preferably two-textured, with a smooth and a rough side; and your smartphone or any other similarly shaped object, for instance a small hardback book or an étui for a pair of eyeglasses. In describing the exercise, I'll use the word "book" to stand for these similarly suitable objects.

Lay the objects out on a table. Do nothing at first—don't touch the objects, don't hold them, don't caress or squeeze them. Doing nothing requires a lot of training. You might be tempted to take the sponge and start doing something with it. Or you might be tempted to judge the sponge without touching it, or judge the exercise without practicing it: "Useless." Doing nothing is more than not engaging in physical actions; it's also not engaging in mental and emotional actions.

The objects are on the table in front of you. Do nothing, to the extent that you can. The best preparation is to do nothing; the best warm-up is to do nothing; you achieve the most by doing the least. To sit with your instrument and to do nothing for a little while—wow. Out of the nothingness in body and mind arise multiple possibilities. To do something means to exclude all other possibilities temporarily. But if you're not doing anything, all possibilities are at your disposal. "Nothing" is "everything in disguise."

The objects are on the table in front of you. Bring your hands toward the objects, but instead of touching them, caress the space right above them—the air, if you will; caress the air above the objects, letting your open palms hover just above the objects. Your imagination and your perception, separately or together, will already gather information about the objects on the table. Without touching anything, you'll know that the objects just below your palms give off different vibes (Figure 8.8).

The objects are on the table in front of you. Now lower your hands millimeter by millimeter until you're touching the objects with your lightest possible touch, piano pianissimo triple and quadruple pianissimo. The alert lightest touch allows you to gather fantastically interesting information about the objects, banal as they may seem at first.

Touch each object in turn. Put the objects side by side, close to one another; lightly touch more than one object with your open palms. Touch the objects with your eyes closed. Your touch sensations are likely to be affected by your seeing or not seeing the objects. Different people react differently to closed and open eyes; it's not guaranteed that you'll have finer touch sensations with your eyes closed, but it's virtually guaranteed that the sensations won't be the same.

> Before I paid attention to the sponge, the sponge was just a sponge. While I was paying attention to the sponge, the sponge was no longer just a sponge. Now that I've absorbed the sponge into my attention, the

Figure 8.8 Object textures. Credit: ©Pedro de Alcantara.

sponge is just a sponge. But what a sponge! What a marvelous object with its special shape and its useful functions, for which I'm so grateful! How incredible that this surface is rough, and this other surface isn't! The sponge is literally two-faced! I love it, despite its two-facedness and because of it!

The enhanced sensitivity will change your piano playing, your cello playing, your oboe playing, your playing of every instrument you'll ever touch. The sponge is just a portal into the world of enriched textural perceptions.

Sponge, kitchen towel. How different they really are! The lightest of touches, and you can tell which is which. There's no confusing the two of them. Handle them, each in turn; change hands, the dominant touching the sponge, the nondominant touching the towel; trade hands. Eyes closed, eyes open. Look, feel; don't look, feel. The hurried and inattentive mind is bored, annoyed, impatient, judgmental. The unhurried and attentive mind is in thrall to fine sensations, to gradations, to the personalities of each object.

And now turn your attention to the third object, the little hardcover book. It's so different from the sponge and the towel—in shape and weight, in color and in function, in feeling, in the emotions it evokes. If you're like me, you might also smell the book, the fresh sponge, and the clean towel. "A book doesn't smell like a sponge." It sounds like a proverb from a wise, ancient culture. It's also a joke, maybe unfunny. It might be part of the lyrics of a song by a clever composer. But the main thing is that these few words encapsulate something important: Different, with a capital D. A sponge, a towel, a book; a teaspoon, a tablespoon, a dessert spoon, a soup spoon; the C string on a cello, the G string, the D, the A: "Different."

Take the kitchen towel and wrap it around the sponge. Touch the double object, handle it, squeeze it. The kitchen towel has a certain texture, which your fingers sense in the touching and squeezing. The sponge has a different texture. It invites and requires a different touch from your hand and fingers. The challenge, then, is for you to have a type of squeezing touch that can sense the towel and its textures, its personality, while also sensing the sponge and its textures, its personality.

Wrap the kitchen towel around the book and repeat the exercise. Put the kitchen towel down and hold the sponge and the book back-to-back; squeeze the double object and sense the double texture. Now make a three-object construction or sandwich: the book and the sponge back-to-back, and the towel enveloping both. Holding and squeezing, train your hands to feel all the textures in the triple object. Each texture needs a different type and degree of squeezing.

Figure 8.9 Hands and fine sand. Credit: Gisela Merkuur.

Figure 8.10 Hands on strings. Credit: Franz P. Sauerteig.

Squeezing the layered towel, sponge, and book, you might imagine that the towel is like skin, the sponge like flesh, and the book like bone: skin, flesh, and bones, layered in sequence. All along these exercises, you are exploring two things at the absolute same time: the objects and your hands themselves. Your hands are layered with their own skin, flesh, and bones. When you hold a three-layered object like the sponge, towel, and book, you can train yourself to feel every layer: those of the objects, those of the hands themselves.

Gradually, suddenly, you might have a revelation about the nature of touch, the intelligence and creativity of your hands, the sheer beauty of the multilayered world (Figures 8.9 and 8.10).

Chapter 9
OBJECT WISDOM
A Manifesto

Your life is made of a constant manipulation of objects of all sorts. Brushing your teeth, you handle a toothbrush with skills acquired in your childhood through trial and error, imitation, and instruction from parents and siblings. Perhaps you take toothbrushing for granted, but it involves complex rotations of arm, wrist, and fingers; the use of the opposable thumb and the other fingers to hold the toothbrush with intelligence and sensitivity; and attention to the toothbrush itself, to the graspability of the handle and the firmness or softness of the bristles. It's a whole microcosm of psychomotor intelligence, not to mention its ritualistic dimensions and its power to evoke deeply held feelings about your teeth, your health, your looks, your family history, and much more besides.

Let's zoom in on the toothbrush as an object. We'll imagine you're using an average old-fashioned toothbrush. It may seem foolish, but compare your toothbrush to a pair of scissors, and you'll be immediately struck by a simple but powerful fact: they're *completely different*, in size, shape, construction, form, function, looks, and materials; they're also completely different in their symbolic dimension and in their presence in your life. They tell different stories (Figures 9.1 and 9.2).

Object Wisdom brings these stories to the forefront of your awareness—the stories that the objects themselves seem to be telling you, although in practice you're telling these stories to yourself and about yourself, prompted by the toothbrush, the scissors, the kitchen knife, the pencil, the flute, the cello, the piano. For the sake of our creative explorations, we'll assign the wisdom to the object itself; we'll convince ourselves in good cheer and without taking things too seriously that the object has a life of its own, that it has stories to tell, and that it wants to share its stories with us and teach us valuable lessons.

Object Wisdom means many things. It means being alert to objects and appreciative of their existence. You have forks and spoons at your disposal, wow! Forks had to be invented, apparently by the Italians during the

Figure 9.1 Pruning shears. Credit: K47.

Figure 9.2 Calligraphy brush. Credit: Thierry Raimbault.

Renaissance; before their invention, you would often eat with your hands or using chunks of bread to bring food from your plate to your mouth. The forks in your kitchen were designed by astute and talented designers, nameless to you but not nameless to themselves and their colleagues at the design studio, and not nameless to their own families and friends. The forks were built using stainless steel, a material that took millennia for humans to create and develop. They were shipped to a nifty store not far from your home. In the absence of an incredibly intricate supply chain, you'd have to fabricate your own forks. Paradox: the fork is banal and not banal at the same time. Object Wisdom acknowledges the paradox, increasing the charge of gratitude and wonderment in your life while letting you go about the business of eating with a fork and a spoon without worrying too much about it.

Object Wisdom is keenly alert to the differences among objects—the difference between a fork and a spoon, which you may think is too obvious to merit mentioning; but also the difference between this fork here and every other fork in the world; the difference between this fork, brand new, and this fork two years from now; the difference between this fork when it's clean and warm and almost steamy coming out of the dishwasher, and this same fork after a messy Thanksgiving dinner. This fork here is a shapeshifter: it doesn't strike us in the same way yesterday and today. Object Wisdom is the art of sensing very fine gradations.

Object Wisdom allows you to discern visible qualities in objects. It allows you to enter a clothing store, scan it quickly, and somehow go toward the one rack where the one linen shirt has been waiting for you. You sort of sense that this rack is wrong, this other rack is wrong for you too, all these racks don't interest you, but—right here, this is the concert shirt I need. Object Wisdom allows you to tell, from one brief touch, if the shirt is made of linen, silk, cotton, or polyester.

At its core, Object Wisdom is probably animistic. Animism is the ancient, perhaps archaic religious attitude that senses a soul in everything: in clouds and rivers and trees, in stones and animals, in names and numbers. Our playful animism considers that every single object has a soul: the shirt, the fork, the cello. This version of animism doesn't have to complicate your practical life (I can't wear this shirt; to the charity shop it goes) or impinge on your churchgoing religious life. All you need is a sort of concentrated alertness to the world and its objects—and, in the alertness, an expression of wonderment and gratitude.

Object Wisdom, playfully or not so playfully, is a dialogue between you and an object. Not a monologue, in which you talk to the shirt and the shirt had better listen to you; not the other monologue, in which the shirt insults you and you're left speechless; not a no-nologue, to coin a term for the total absence of conversation; but a true back-and-forth in which you listen to the fork, the shirt, and the concert grand, and the concert grand listens to you.

The objects don't necessarily talk in English or other known languages; they don't necessarily speak in complete paragraphs; they don't necessarily have an agenda to discuss with you. Rather, they have intrinsic qualities or possibilities that propagate outwardly. The linen shirt is asking you to pay attention, to feel and sense, to try it on, to inhabit it, to allow it to envelop you and caress you and protect you from the elements, to allow it to elevate your presence in your own eyes and in the eyes of others. Then you wear the shirt and you think to yourself, "This shirt is my friend" (Figure 9.3).

Object Wisdom is a discipline, in the sense of a committed and constant practice over the long term. Your home is a perfect territory for the practice, regardless of what your home is like. The rehearsal studio is perfect. The city is perfect. A toothbrush is perfect as a study in all the implications of Object Wisdom. The discipline implies many things, but first and foremost a foundational attitude: attentiveness, wonderment, gratitude. To this, we may add a sense of obligation and duty. Your objects require and deserve your attention. If your cello doesn't like humidity, it's your duty to install a dehumidifier in

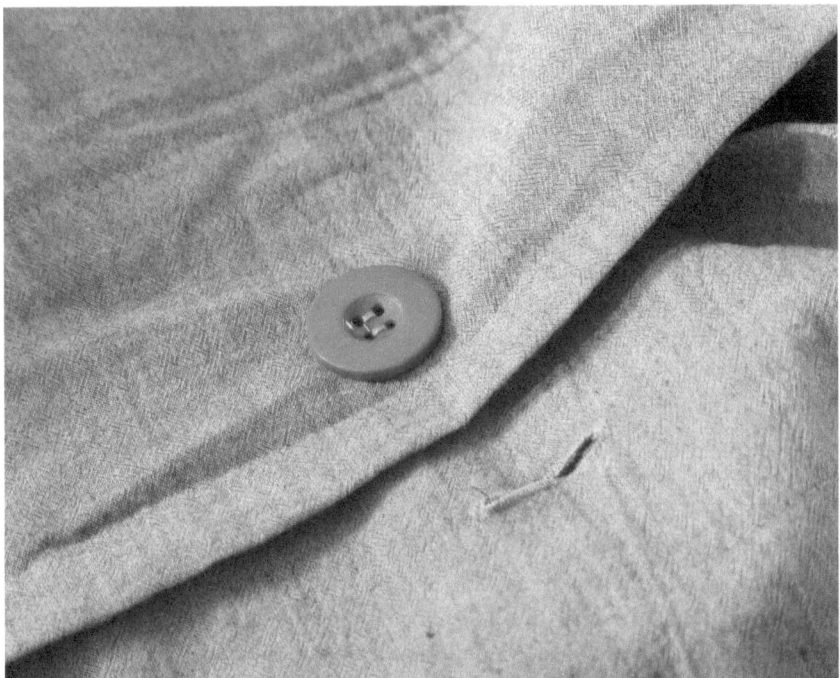

Figure 9.3 Fabric and button. Credit: yaoyaoyao5yaoyaoyao.

the room where your cello lives. And if your cello doesn't like dryness, it's your duty to keep it hydrated. Paradox: your instrument is both an elevated herald of divine voices, and a practical tool for everyday purposes. You risk not using the instrument if you over-elevate it in your estimation. Decades ago, my grandmother gave my mother a raincoat. Then she told my mother not to wear it in the rain because the coat would get wet. A new rug? Don't step on it! A new flute? Don't salivate on it!

Object Wisdom acknowledges the imperfectness of the human being. I'll scratch the cello sooner or later. I'll rip the shirt by accident. I'll drop the flute, and I'll regret it, and I'll pay a cost that is both emotional and financial. But the terror at the faint probability of dropping the flute could make it difficult for you to play the flute. You may not be completely conscious of it, but the fear of risks, real and imagined, affects yourself, your whole body, and of course your hands, wrists, and fingers. You hold on tight to the instrument because otherwise you'll drop it. Issues of control are so big in life and in music making that we're justified in using a capital letter: Control. To meditate on Control and what it means to you, it's useful to willingly drop an object that suffers no ill effects from being dropped. We'll incorporate this into our disciplined practice of Object Wisdom.

Object Wisdom doesn't mean never making mistakes or hurting an object. It means recovering from the mistakes and the hurt; it means repairing objects that need repairing; it means talking to your own sweet self with compassion after you make the costly mistake of dropping the object or dropping something inside the object (a coffee cup into the piano). Object Wisdom has technicians, friends and colleagues, healers and guides at your disposal.

Object Wisdom means watching other people handle objects and marveling at the perfectly poised child rushing by on a scooter, or the perfectly skillful woodworker making a perfect cut on a perfect piece of wood. Marveling at others is good for your hands, wrists, and fingers; envying others and wishing them ill is bad for your hands, wrists, and fingers (Figure 9.4).

Object Wisdom isn't literal-minded. When you see someone juggle five balls without effort, you don't need to think that you must learn how to juggle five balls without effort. Instead, you look at the juggler and think that you'd like to do things with less effort—all things, including slicing a tomato or opening a package. Or playing the cello and the oboe and the guitar. Literal-mindedness makes your mind stiff and your wrists stiff. Watch the juggler, observe and absorb the dimension of flow, of letting go, of being attentive and lighthearted; then play the cello. Juggling contains two types of skills: the specific and the universal. You might not be able to apply the specifics to cello playing, but you'd certainly be able to apply the universals.

Figure 9.4 Drawknife. Credit: Graham Hobster.

Object Wisdom makes room for everyone. You don't have Object Wisdom; it's the object that has wisdom and imparts it to you. You can be a complete beginner in the art; you can be the most awkward beginner ever born (although you almost certainly are not); you can hate objects and hate wisdom; still, you belong with Object Wisdom, because to be alive is to have a relationship with objects. You don't acquire skills first and then join the club; you belong to the club already, whether you applied for admission or not. It's a dangerous mind that refuses to acknowledge the existence of Object Wisdom (Figure 9.5).

The Instrument as Archetype

We'll imagine (without regard to facts or numbers) that there's a deity, eternal and infinite, called Keyboard. Now we'll imagine and perceive, then believe and affirm, that every keyboard is the child of Keyboard the deity. A computer keyboard is a cousin, distant or not so distant, of the keyboard of a concert grand. The acceptance of Keyboard and her Children allows you to free your mind and your body (and your hands, wrists, and fingers) from the Specialization Syndrome, the state of self in which you believe yourself incapable of doing anything other than this one thing that you do already: "I'm a

Figure 9.5 Hands of music. Credit: Bea Hutchins.

pianist; I play the piano; I don't play the harpsichord or the clavichord, never have, never will."

This is the "Never; Don't!" voice of the stinky underworld trying to determine your life, your behaviors, your likes and dislikes, and ultimately your health. I don't mean that you must be or become a great pianist and a great harpsichordist and a great organist, good and great and perfect across the board. I mean that you might want to free your mind of the "Never; Don't!" voice. Then you can approach varied instruments with curiosity and pleasure: "This piano is a child of Keyboard; this clavichord is a child of Keyboard; I'm familiar with Keyboard, and I enjoy meeting her children."

Every flute is a child of Flute: the silver flute, the traverso, the bansuri, the piccolo, the alto, the nose flute, the ocarina, the pan flute, the tin whistle. How many flutes has Flute begotten? It's an uncountable number. Every bowed instrument is a child of Violin: the fiddle, the rebec, the viola, the cello, the viola d'amore, the double bass, the gamba, the gadulka, the jinghu, the byzaanchy. Every trumpet and cornet; every drum and tambourine; every guitar and zither: every instrument is the child of a fecund and nondenominational deity (Figures 9.6, 9.7, and 9.8).

Let's say that a pianist approaches a particular piano for the first time. For the sake of discussion, we'll name it "the piano-other," which is and isn't the same as "the other piano." The piano-other is fundamentally different from

Figure 9.6 Tree of flutes. Credit: Arjun Jaisawal.

Figure 9.7 Pan flute. Credit: StockSnap.

Figure 9.8 Silver flute. Credit: José Arroyo.

the piano-self. Rigid mind and fingers approach the piano-other in a certain way; fluid mind and fingers approach it in another way. If you're set to habit, your first touch when playing the piano-other creates a clash. You aren't really exploring the piano-other; instead, you're unconsciously set to touch your own piano, which we call the piano-self. You'll blame the piano-other for the clash, and you'll issue an expedited judgment: crappy, horrible, hellish. "This thing is hurting me, it's hurting my ears, it's hurting my fingers."

If you see an instrument as the manifestation of an archetype (or, as we've put it, the child of a deity), you approach it without preconceptions. "This isn't a piano or the piano; this is Piano, a child of Keyboard. I want to play with it."

You don't need to master every instrument; mastery isn't part of my argument. Three notes played on the piano-other (or the cello-other, the guitar-other), and your experience may be sufficient: you had a taste. Ten notes, and you may receive an inkling of a possibility: the soundtrack to an indie horror movie. It doesn't matter if the inkling is a musical cliché; what matters is that you had a creative response to the situation. Five minutes, and your soundtrack becomes more meaningful, to you and to potential listeners. It's possible that the piano-other is uniquely suited to certain musical tasks; it's possible that you might not have captured these possibilities before touching the instrument; it's possible that you didn't capture these possibilities after playing the first three notes.

Hello, Old Joe; Goodbye, Old Joe

Each instrument offers its own possibilities. A given instrument may be able to offer you dozens and dozens of sounds, techniques, aesthetics, timbres. Another instrument may have a narrower range of potentialities. But keep five things in mind:

1. Each instrument is individual, and each instrument is an individual.
2. There can be deep differences between apparently similar instruments.
3. There are deep differences between different instrumentalists.
4. The same instrument doesn't sound alike in the hands of different players.
5. Assessing an instrument's potentialities isn't always straightforward.

Play as many different instruments as you can: those of your colleagues, friends, and students; those in shops and public spaces. Borrow someone else's instrument for a concert. Handle the strange, the new, the different, the foreign. Handle the wrong instrument, or seemingly wrong.

Take the exploration to extremes. Somewhere—the basement in your neighbor's house—there's an abandoned upright piano that hasn't been played in 50 years: dusty and rusty Old Joe. Go visit him. It doesn't matter how out of tune, how broken, how mechanically outdated; the instrument is its own self; it offers you sounds and experiences that a concert grand can't provide. If you try to impose upon Old Joe your version of Rachmaninoff's Second Piano Concerto, the results could be frustrating to you and to Old Joe (Figure 9.9).

Sit with Old Joe and witness his history and personality; witness his abused and insulted body; witness his voice, muffled and stifled; touch his keys lightly with the sensitive pads of your fingertips, running your fingers along the keys without pressing them down, sensing the difference between keys with no action left in them and keys with a faint spark of life, sensing the difference between keys with missing bits and keys still whole.

It's possible you'll be touching ivory for the first time in your life, and possibly for the last time as well. The ivory comes from the tusk of an elephant slaughtered a hundred years earlier; ivory piano keys are an ethical and environmental disaster, and they have been rightly banned. But here you are, touching something that is at the same time banal and special, objectionable and yet amazing. The experience educates your touch; the entire experience, including the basement, the neighbor, the dust, the cobwebs, the muffled

Figure 9.9 Old Joe. Credit: Peter H.

sounds, the intonation: not a single piano in the history of humanity has looked and sounded exactly like this piano.

Between the most exquisite concert grand and Old Joe there are thousands of pianos of wide-ranging personalities. You don't need to play thousands of different pianos, or even hundreds or dozens; it's enough that you make yourself available for playing with and on instruments other than your habitual ones. True availability comes without preconceived ideas, assumptions, or judgments. Old Joe isn't a pile of worthless junk; it becomes so in your mind and your heart. Perhaps your fingers recoil upon touching it, or your fingers recoil at the thought of touching it or at the memory of having touched it. Finger recoil is heart recoil. Do it often enough, and you'll give yourself heart problems and finger problems.

For some people, their instrument is a source of joy and wonderment; for others, it's more like a source of obligations, frustrations, and painful memories including episodes of embarrassment or humiliation. There are instrumentalists who own and play a single instrument; there are instrumentalists with a collector's streak who keep multiple instruments going. In many homes, there lies an untouched guitar, an untouched piano, an untouched flute not played in many years because—no, it's too painful to talk about it. "Are you willing to help me take Old Joe to the city dump?" "Sure. Let me finish saying goodbye to him."

The practice of Object Wisdom alters your musical aesthetics. A cellist I know from my youth once bought an expensive Italian cello. He made the purchase impulsively, borrowing a fair amount of money to pay for it. I'd say he bought the instrument not knowing it well, and probably not knowing his own self well, his aspirations and blind spots. He assumed, or he hoped, that the instrument was objectively good in itself—that is, independently of the behavior of the player.

Then the struggles started.

The cello wouldn't respond to his commands. My colleague had strong ideas about sound, and he wanted his new cello to make the exact sounds that he brought forth from his imagination. The struggle came with buyer's regret, but also with serious aches and pains. At some point, my colleague saw the light, and he sensed and understood that the instrument had its own voice, or even many voices, and his job as a cellist was to let the cello speak and sing as it wanted to speak and sing. His pains dissipated, and he made his peace with the cello and with the seemingly risky impulsive purchase.

Ideally, Object Wisdom would help you test an instrument before buying it. But Object Wisdom can also help you mend a difficult relationship after an instrument enters your life.

The Player of All Instruments

Some people define a pianist as a talented, highly trained, accomplished concert artist. "Oh, no; I'm not a pianist; I just play the piano." For some other people, to be a pianist means to play the piano, however well or poorly. An adult amateur beginner, perhaps untrained, inattentive, and—for the sake of argument—untalented: at the piano, playing one note tentatively, our friend is a pianist. And for some other people still, being a pianist is an inner state of potentialities. A newborn is a pianist already, even though he or she has yet to take a first breath and let out a first cry. The littlest of little kids loves going to the piano, standing next to it, touching its surfaces, noticing her reflections on the shiny surface of the piano; the littlest of the little, held in the arms of a loving parent who's sitting at the piano, reaches out and caresses a key; the littlest of the little has proved to the world that she's a pianist.

Object Wisdom loves little kids who "know nothing" (Figure 9.10).

A story is told of Hermeto Pascoal, the great Brazilian multi-instrumentalist, composer, improviser, and arranger. The story may be apocryphal, but we'll take it as symbolic and meaningful. Pascoal was born in 1936 in the Brazilian hinterlands. As an adolescent, he moved to Rio de Janeiro, then the country's capital, arriving in the big city with no money and no friends. Out in the streets, he bumped into someone whose middle name may have been Providence: "I'm playing in a bar tonight. We need a bass player. How

Figure 9.10 Wisdom of naiveté. Credit: thedanw.

about you join us?" "Sure, I'd love to." Pascoal had never played the bass, but it didn't matter. He learned it on the spot, by doing it; the story (apocryphal, maybe!) says that he played all night until his fingers bled.

A pit musician at a Broadway musical, able to pass from the flute to the clarinet to the saxophone. A keyboard player, able to play the piano, the fortepiano, the harpsichord, the clavichord, and the organ. Or a pianist, able to play uprights, baby grands, concert grands, toy pianos, familiar pianos, and unfamiliar pianos. A violinist who also plays the viola. A cellist who plays the modern cello, the Baroque cello, and the five-string cello. A multi-instrumentalist, able to play the cello, the guitar, the piano, and the Native American flute. A flutist who plays the piccolo, the alto, the bass flute, the traverso, and the bansuri. Examples abound, with a shared principle: adaptability. The adaptability is total, involving aesthetics, perception, sensorial responses, and of course the behavior of the hands, wrists, and fingers.

For the sake of argument, we'll call the woodwind player at the Broadway musical a generalist, and we'll call the flutist who only plays one instrument a specialist. Two different mindsets, two different personalities and aesthetics, two different goals in life, two different musicians. I'm not saying that a specialist should become a generalist; rather, I think that if you're a specialist, you might want to have a "latent generalist" inside yourself—a sort of quality in reserve, a possibility of adaptation which you may use or not.

"Pedro, how many instruments do you play?"

Figure 9.11 Object wisdom and poise. Credit: ymyphoto.

"All of them, without exception."

I don't claim to play them well, appropriately, or acceptably. I might handle an oboe without blowing into it, instead producing faint clicking sounds by pressing on its keys a few times: "I'm playing the oboe." Once you make the distinction between being an excellent professional oboist and playing the oboe, you can play the oboe and let your open mind, your glad heart, and your curious fingers explore every instrument and learn useful things from the exploration.

You may be a "No!" kind of musician or a "Yes!" kind of musician. Object Wisdom probably thinks that "No!" is a problem, for which "Yes!" may be a solution. Go talk to Object Wisdom and find out for yourself (Figure 9.11).

Chapter 10

OBJECT WISDOM

A Workshop

Juggling Balls

Get two or more soft juggling balls. They're easy to buy on the Internet and elsewhere. Juggling balls have so many useful qualities that every musician and every music teacher should stock up on them. We won't be learning how to juggle, even though juggling does offer many learning opportunities. Instead, we'll use them to explore texture, shape, size, form, function, intrinsic qualities, specifics and universals.

1. Every game in Object Wisdom starts with no rules. You're given a toy without the instruction manual. The first learning experience isn't to learn something but to agree not to know what you're supposed to be doing or how you should be doing it. Handle the object as if it's an incomprehensible artifact from a faraway culture.
2. To an adult, household objects are normal, logical, ordinary. They've always been there. But for a baby, every object is new and perhaps incomprehensible. Sooner or later, a strange object becomes a lamp, but to begin with, it's a thing or an entity or a source of miracles, light and heat, shadows, sounds, stories.
3. The problem with knowing too soon is that knowledge prevents or eliminates discovery. A banal object discovered for the first time can be very exciting—because discovery is a sudden flow of energy, a sudden perception, a sudden realization.
4. Another problem comes when analytical or intellectual knowledge tries to usurp sensorial knowledge. You know this thing is a juggling ball; you've seen it, you know what it's used for; you know that the outer shell is made of pieces of vinyl or imitation leather; you know that the filling is made of birdseed or sand or some other similar material.

5. But have you sensed the object's textures? Have you pushed a juggling ball against your cheek and received its loving kiss? Have you rolled a juggling ball along your neck and received its healing massage? Have you placed a juggling ball under your armpit and felt how it changed the shape of your body, opening your chest and ribcage?
6. You can be *absolutely certain* that you know something, but events, circumstances, a person, a book, or an Internet search can prove you wrong. Then your absolute certainty is shattered, and you'll need to choose between laughing at yourself or resenting the Internet search or the person that proved you wrong.
7. Absolute certainty hurts your hands, wrists, and fingers; being wrong without knowing that you're wrong hurts your hands, wrists, and fingers; resentment is fatal to your hands, wrists, and fingers.
8. Juggling balls: ignorance and discovery. You really don't know yet what you'll do with the balls. The instruction manual is being written second by second as you handle the balls. The touch of "I don't know yet" is very different from the touch of "I know already" (Figure 10.1).
9. Handling a juggling ball, you'll be struck by a seemingly banal fact: the ball is round, though not perfectly round like a steel ball used in a

Figure 10.1 Juggling balls. Credit: ©Pedro de Alcantara.

ball-bearing wheel. Your hands must not—*must not!*—chide the ball for not being perfectly round. To put it differently, each object is what it is. And the hands of wisdom perceive what is, free from suppositions and judgments.

10. Oh, how squeezable this thing is! Sit quietly somewhere with one or two juggling balls in your hands and squeeze them, with no purpose other than enjoying the available sensations. It's possible that you'll start daydreaming and hallucinating a little. You might visit a problem in your mind; you might receive a solution to a problem. A squeezable object invites many emotions.

11. Look at the object. Shapes and colors, a shiny surface, stitches. Let the collector in you become wistful or acquisitive: fifteen or twenty juggling balls, no two exactly alike; I could display them in some clever way, maybe lined up on top of my piano; I'd be in a good mood every time I practiced.

12. A juggling ball has many cousins: tangerines, mandarins, satsumas, oranges, and limes, to name just a few similarly shaped objects. You could do this whole exercise with tangerines. Tennis balls, softballs, and baseballs would work, too (Figures 10.2 and 10.3).

13. Now sit at a table or stand by a countertop. Put one juggling ball on the table. The ball is just sitting there, minding its own business. Thanks to our informal animism, we feel that objects have personalities, feelings, intentions, and stories to tell. And long ago, we convinced ourselves that being silly and overimaginative was good for our hands, wrists, and fingers.

14. Your job isn't to play with the ball yet, but only to witness the ball being its sweet self. Etymologically, the word "witness" comes from an old root meaning "to see (and, metaphorically, to know)." Other words that spring from the same root include "advice, clairvoyant, supervise, improvise." We'll learn a lot from witnessing a juggling ball doing nothing. It'll prepare us to witness the piano or the harp doing nothing, therefore preparing us to play the piano or the harp in some very special ways.

15. When witnessing, we have no objectives, no agenda. The hands, wrists, and fingers of no-agenda have a particular freedom. It's with this freedom that we now touch the juggling ball. We don't grab it or hold it or squeeze it; we touch it as softly as we can. We want to become able to pass from no touch to a minimal touch almost indistinguishable from no touch. In the abstract, a perfect range of gradations might go from zero to one thousand. Mastery requires that we become able to pass from zero to one, from one to two, and so on.

Figure 10.2 Tennis ball. Credit: StockSnap.

Figure 10.3 Baseball. Credit: Francisco Corado Rivera.

16. With the lightest touch, push the ball a little and see if it budges. How much pressure do you need to apply so that the ball budges? You're training yourself to play the piano or the guitar with sensitive hands that can go from zero to one to two, to five, to fifteen, on that famous scale of gradations that goes up to one thousand.
17. With one hand on the juggling ball, we increase our force so that the ball rolls on the table. Our play accelerates, the movements become bigger; we roll the ball, we push the ball, we play, we play, we play.
18. The ball rolls. This is another fact that is far from banal, because the ball is teaching us about shapes, surfaces, and potential movements. In time, we'll expand the experience into a bigger principle: Each object has its potential movements.
19. Lay a hand flat, with the palm facing upward. Use your other hand to drop the ball onto the open palm from close range. Can you receive the falling ball without grabbing and gripping? Can your open hand stay neutral? Can you receive something without trying to control it?
20. Let's throw the ball from hand to hand. Speed, rhythm, amplitude, gesture; initiative, risk-taking, technique, pleasure. The juggling ball is friendly to the thrower and friendly to the catcher. A heavy spiked metal ball wouldn't be so friendly. Therefore, we feel gratitude toward our friend the soft juggling ball, and our game now has a name: "Gratitude."
21. No, you're not going to claim that you're no good at sports and don't know how to play the game, and you hate throwing and catching, and you're afraid of screwing it up, and the ball will hit the vase and break it, and it's a mess, and it's your fault, Pedro. No. Instead, you'll practice and play, take it easy and play, spend time with the juggling ball and play. The hands of "it's your fault, Pedro" are very different from the hands of "practice and play." Mozart broke a vase. Clara Schumann broke a vase. Charlie Parker broke a vase or three. Karlheinz Stockhausen broke a vase or seventeen.
22. There are a lot of variables in throwing and catching. How far apart or how close are your hands? How hard or how softly do you throw? How much time do you allow between throws? How are you going to direct your head, neck, back, and shoulders?
23. Get a steady rhythm going. Throw and catch for a minute or longer. While playing, improvise a scatting song with rhythms that coincide with the rhythms of your game. Throwing and catching now have a linguistic dimension.
24. Throw the ball somewhere out of your reach—across the room, for instance. This is a game of throw and catch without catching. In its infinite wisdom, the ball is teaching you how to relax and let go, how to

subvert a game's rules (in this case, the obligation to catch every throw). Throw the ball; let it fall where it will; now go answer emails or take a nap.

The Book

When my grandfather passed away, I was given the opportunity of choosing a few of his objects as keepsakes. The items I gathered included a tiny ivory Buddha, a letter opener that looks like a dagger, and two syringe metal containers. My grandfather was a pediatrician, and these containers were part of his work life. The containers are plain, seemingly ordinary; they aren't jewel-encrusted fancy boxes from a royal household. But they're perfect in themselves, perfectly proportioned, perfectly suited to their purposes. They make me think of Bauhaus, the art and design school founded by Walter Gropius (1883–1969) in Weimar, Germany. The Bauhaus aesthetics aimed to merge art, craft, and industry. It valued functionality and minimalism; objects and buildings were streamlined and void of ornamentation. Symbolically and emotionally, my grandfather's syringe containers are more valuable than the jewel-encrusted royal box of our imagination (Figure 10.4).

Figure 10.4 Cherished objects. Credit: ©Pedro de Alcantara.

I'd be quite upset if I lost these boxes, if a visitor stole one or both, or if someone put a dent on them. Ultimately, they're sacred to me; and because they're sacred to me, I believe that they're sacred "in themselves." The amalgamation of a thing and your feelings about a thing is a well-known phenomenon. It's useful to acknowledge it, to observe its workings in your life, and to integrate the phenomenon into your quest for fulfillment.

You can probably throw away a beat-up toothbrush without too much thought, but can you throw away the keepsakes that represent your childhood, your family history, your roots, your aspirations, your hopes, your fears? Creative Health is full of paradoxes. Creative Health sees a soul in a coffee mug or in a syringe box, and you must honor their souls. But to grow and learn, you must handle objects without fussiness. If breaking a coffee mug somehow gets you to play the piano better, break it you must! Your hands, wrists, and fingers have their rights and privileges, which sometimes are greater than the rights and privileges of objects.

Many people consider that a book has a special place in the pantheon of objects. It can be difficult for us to mark a book up with pencil or with pen, or—heaven forbid!—with a marker. If you accidentally rip a little corner of a page somewhere inside the book, this hurts you more than it hurts the book. The fear of maiming a book affects your hands, wrists, and fingers. The fear might make them smarter or dumber; nothing is guaranteed. But for this Object Wisdom exercise, you must agree to hurt a book, possibly, maybe; nothing is guaranteed.

We'll ponder the book as an object, independent of the text and images that the book contains. For this exercise and meditation, use two paperbacks of similar sizes. You'll be handling the books in many ways, and it's not impossible that one or both books will be damaged in the process: a torn page, a broken spine. You'll work better if the books you choose for the exercise can suffer these indignities without your worrying too much.

Forget about the text and images, forget about the book as a carrier of printed information. Handle your book as you would a box, a piece of fruit, or a trinket. This may be a challenge for some people, who think that "a book is a book." Pass it from hand to hand, feel its shape and weight, its edges. Do you like the smell of paper? I do, too. The physicality of the book is there to give your hands, wrists, and fingers (and your nose) a lot of pleasure.

Flip through the book's pages. I know you've done this countless times in your life. But the frame of mind of Object Wisdom alters your perception of ordinary actions and infuses your actions with renewed energy. Holding the book with the purpose of flipping through its pages is very different from simply holding the book. Your hands light up in a particular manner. One hand holds the book, readying it for the operation. The other flips through

Figure 10.5 Page flipping. Credit: Petra.

the pages, with the thumb in charge of sensing the pages and controlling their behavior (Figure 10.5).

Flipping is a musical action, with variations of dynamics and tempo. In less than a second, flip through all pages, presto prestissimo. Now decide to flip page by page through the whole book, however long it takes you to accomplish the task: andante molto moderato. A single page, and your thumb is in control, intimately connected with the page and its placement in the book. Look at the page numbers as you flip through them. Your eyes, eager not to miss a single page number, prod the thumb to exert fine control. Hold the book close to one of your ears: the sound of pages flipping is a lovely caress. Habitually, we tend to flip the pages with our dominant hand. Change hands and flip the pages with your nondominant hand. It's a whole other ballgame.

What can you do with a book other than read it? Sit on it, use the book as a headdress to improve your posture, hold the book under your armpit to feel the dialogue between the underarm and the trunk. Imagination, curiosity, and humor will lead you to invent new uses for a book. And each novelty will entertain and educate your hands, wrists, and fingers.

If your book is a paperback, it has a built-in suppleness missing from a hardback. Holding the book by its spine end, swing it at different speeds and different ranges of motion. The book will make interesting sound effects, like a strange percussion instrument. Control of the strange instrument is control of your hands, wrists, and fingers. Two hands, two paperback books, two instruments making music, two objects imparting their wisdom to you.

The Thread

Gather a few jars with lids and bottles with threaded caps. Other objects with threads are good, too—for instance, a toothpaste tube.

The thread is a marvel of ingenuity and design. It's very practical, allowing us to open and close jars and bottles. It exists in a variety of types, for instance the childproof thread in a medicine container. But we'll leave industrial and commercial considerations aside, and we'll ponder the thread as a path or channel, as a connection between two surfaces, as an invitation to move along a predetermined groove. And we'll take note of the spiral shape of the path (Figure 10.6).

From the objects that you've gathered, choose a jar. For the sake of describing the exercise, we'll say that you have a medium-sized glass jar, washed clean, together with its lid. You might be tempted to open and close the jar, but it'd be good for you to handle the jar and lid as a unit, to sense the object's shape, size, and weight, to look at it as a sort of work of art, to bring it close to your eyes, and to see how light passes through the jar and creates interesting visual distortions.

Hold the jar with one hand and wrap your other hand around the lid. Just that: wrap the hand and don't try to open the jar. It takes self-control to

Figure 10.6 Thread. Credit: congerdesign.

postpone a goal when the goal is already in your hands. But by not opening and not trying to open the jar, you can better sense the object and its construction. This will be helpful when the time comes to open the jar.

Now open the jar. There are at least four ways of doing it:

1. Hold the jar with your dominant hand. Turn and open the lid with the other hand.
2. Trade hands.
3. Hold the lid with your dominant hand. Use the other hand to turn the jar until it separates from the lid.
4. Trade hands.

How much effort do you need to open the jar? Test gradations of muscle power until you open and close the jar with the least possible exertion. Struggling with a lid, many people unwittingly press the sides of the lid into the thread; they aren't looking for the movement along the thread but choking the lid.

Open the jar partway. Close it again, then move the lid back and forth. Are your fingers alone doing the work, or are you engaging your hands, the wrists, and perhaps forearms as well? My question doesn't imply that it's wrong to engage your forearms. It all depends. The main thing is that the intelligent spiral paths in the threads invite intelligent rotations in your arms and hands.

Does the lid make sounds as it travels along the thread? I bet it does. Do you enjoy the sounds? Object Wisdom incites pleasure in all the sensations triggered by all objects.

Alternate your explorations among all the objects you gathered for the exercise. Different sizes and shapes, different paths; a bottle cap might require three or four full rotations to open, while a honey jar might require only half a rotation.

Our general principle says that activities have specific characteristics and universal characteristics. Opening a jar doesn't have the same specifics as plucking the strings of a guitar. But both activities involve touch, rotation, sensitivity, intelligence, attention, and many other shared dimensions. The attentive jar opener becomes the attentive string plucker.

A Stick of Wood

For your next Object Wisdom exploration, you need a stick of wood, something like the handle of a small broom. The first challenge is to find the "right" stick of wood for the exploration. I use quotation marks because the true first challenge in creative exploration is to take it easy as regards right and wrong. There are two types of creative explorers. One insists on high standards, quality materials, useful procedures, and solid outcomes. The other insists on curiosity, adaptability, and the marvels of the unknown, the unexpected, and the uncontrolled. Both explorers have their talents and their blind spots. I think it's interesting to engage in a play of opposing forces between these two perspectives. To have a specific marvelous object in your hands is marvelous; to do something marvelous with whatever is in your hands is marvelous.

Go find some stick of wood, perhaps half a broom stick, perhaps the skinny leg of a wooden table that a neighbor is dumping in the garbage. A stick of wood, my kingdom for a stick of wood!

In the mind of the alert child, a stick of wood can be anything and everything: a sword, a baseball bat, a totem, a magic wand; something to hit surfaces and make noises with, something to poke sleeping bears and make enemies with. And it can also be a silent oboe, a magic flute, a crazy clarinet, a skeletal bassoon, a conductor's baton.

Here you are, alert and curious, handling a stick of wood with clever hands, wrists, and fingers. Poke the bear. Hit a pillow. Twirl the stick. Find the stick's center of gravity and hold the stick horizontally, in balance; your fingers need to do almost nothing because the stick is in equilibrium.

The stick is both a wonderful thing to play with and potential garbage. What happens if you drop the stick? Nothing. The stick "doesn't mind it." If you drop your real oboe, the oboe minds it a great deal. But the stick silently invites you to drop it on the floor, on a carpet, or on a couch. Naughty children will drop it out of the window, onto an empty sidewalk. Very naughty children will drop it from a bridge into a river 20 meters below.

The stick is a symbol of freedom, an invitation to carefreeness. Your hands, wrists, and fingers develop a particular energy when handling the Stick of Freedom, which is a source of Object Wisdom. And, with those clever, alert playful hands, you can then play the oboe or the clarinet (Figure 10.7).

Integration

A philosopher, a psychoanalyst, a sculptor, and a shaman meet at a conference, where they participate in a round table with the task of defining the word "object." We too give up on the impossible task of defining something so kaleidoscopic. Instead, we make a short, informal, incomplete list of certain types of objects that we're used to handling.

1. Kitchenware: knives, forks, spoons, peelers, cups, plates, bowls, sponges.
2. Toolbox: hammers, screwdrivers, nails, screws, wrenches, pliers.
3. Bathroom cabinet: toothbrushes, Q-tips, soap dispensers, loofahs, nail clippers.
4. Office supplies: pencils, pens, notebooks, paperclips, erasers, rulers, scissors.

Figure 10.7 Flute. Credit: Rijksmuseum.

5. Bookshelf: knickknacks, bobbleheads, candlesticks. Ah, yes, books.
6. Assorted: yo-yos, rubber duckies, harmonicas, finger puppets.
7. Music studio: music stands, metronomes, tuning forks, scores, mementos.
8. Cello case: cello, bow, rosin, mute, earplugs, chamois cloth.

The left brain calls it a numbered list of disparate things; the right brain calls it a head trip, where the cellist is going through the house looking at everything, touching everything, testing everything, playing with everything, and absorbing the wisdom of every object, *every single object*. Object Wisdom is synonymous with Life (Figures 10.8, 10.9, 10.10, and 10.11).

Figure 10.8 Handle. Credit: Ornella Sannazzaro.

Figure 10.9 Guitar. Credit: bustaluiggi.

Figure 10.10 Pen. Credit: Rijksmuseum.

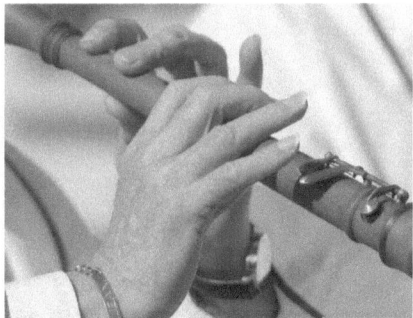

Figure 10.11 Wind instrument. Credit: Jacqueline Macou.

Chapter 11

STRENGTH REDEFINED

How you define the notion of strength will predetermine how you use your hands, wrists, and fingers.

R. Buckminster Fuller (1895–1983) was an American architect, inventor, and visionary. Like all visionaries, he had many ideas that were too far ahead of his time; ideas that seemed good and wonderful but were impossible to put into practice; and foolish and crazy ideas, too. But some of his ideas were given durable shape. He was interested in geodesic domes: hemispherical structures constructed with lattices of rigid triangular elements. Many such domes have been built around the world as auditoriums, greenhouses, sports arenas, storage facilities, and public art. Geodesic domes are surprisingly strong and stable structures, and they can withstand heavy loads relative to their size (Figure 11.1).

Explaining how it works would leave most of us confused and discouraged, besides not being necessary for our purposes. Instead, let's fast-forward from Buckminster Fuller to structural strength to *tensegrity*, which is an abbreviation of *tensional integrity*. Tensegrity, or a harmony of tensions, is one of the reasons why a geodesic dome is strong and stable. It appears that Buckminster Fuller himself coined the term in 1955, though sometimes it's said that the sculptor Kenneth Snelson (1927–2016), who studied with Fuller in the 1940s, is the term's conceptual godfather. Snelson's work is highly varied. Among other things, it includes beautiful sculptures, some small and some very large, using cables and pipes in intricate combinations. The cables pull on the pipes, the pipes resist their pulls; the entire object is strong and stable. The triangular components that, in a lattice, create a geodesic dome are only one of the possible building blocks of tensegrity structures, as the cables and pipes of Snelson's sculptures demonstrate (Figure 11.2).

Over the decades, the concept of tensegrity spread its wings and came to be explored in a variety of fields beyond engineering, architecture, and art. Stephen M. Levin, MD is credited with having coined the term *biotensegrity* in a bid to create a new understanding of human functioning. Buildings, sculptures, and human beings, then, may all be considered tensegrity structures if

Figure 11.1 Geodesic dome. Credit: Eduardo Ponce de Leon.

Figure 11.2 Tensegrity structure. Credit: commons.wikimedia.org.

they contain certain characteristics, of which the most important is a balance of necessary tensions.

1. Although this fact seems banal, it's worth keeping in mind that every part of your body is connected to the whole: each part is connected to all other parts. There's a continuous path from your toenail to the crown of your head, and indeed from any one point to any other point. In a spiderweb, all strands are delicately connected. The spider knows immediately when a fly has landed in the web, however far the spider may be from the landing spot. This is the reality of your body, although your perception may not be as fine as a spider's. Improving your perception starts with embracing the very notion of interconnectedness of all parts.
2. Every point in your body is in constant silent dialogue with all other points. Imagine your body as a tree strung with lights, maybe a thousand little lights shining or not shining as needed, but always ready to shine. You touch one piano key with one finger, but beyond the fingertip there are a thousand points of light participating not in movement and effort, but in alertness and energy. If all points are working together, no point needs to work hard. You might then feel that you're completely relaxed when in fact you're doing everything that you need to do to feel that you're completely connected.
3. The participation of points may involve movement, but there's also participation in resistance, support, and counterbalance. You don't need to move everything, and most of the time you'll be more comfortable not moving everything all the time. A thousand people at the assembly, all of them ready, none of them asleep. They don't have to talk all at the same time.
4. Distributed resistance is key to strength. Imagine that you must carry a heavy weight on your head or over your shoulders. If you don't resist the weight-bearing down upon your head and neck, you'll crumple under the weight and hurt yourself. If you try to resist the weight with your head and neck only, or perhaps with your shoulders, you'll stiffen the neck and shoulders, hurting yourself again. Have every point at your disposal; have every point do at least a tiny little bit of work; have every point ready to offer resistance and support; and have every point ready to move if movement is necessary, and ready to remain still if stillness is necessary (Figures 11.3, 11.4, 11.5, and 11.6).
5. Stand near a wall, door, bookshelf, or a similar surface. An average standing posture would be fine. Or tweak your posture and make it resemble a sort of martial art attitude: one foot a few inches ahead of

Figure 11.3 Distributed resistance. Credit: Nur Aziz Arifin.

Figure 11.4 Resistance and poise. Credit: Artsy Solomon.

Figure 11.5 Resistance, poise, and love. Credit: Tamotoji.

Figure 11.6 Resistance and connection. Credit: Chris Thornton.

the other, the body leaning forward very slightly from the ankle joint. Now raise an arm and touch the wall with the tip of your dominant index finger. You're essentially pointing at the wall, but with no distance between your finger and the wall; your body is a sort of bridge from the floor to the wall. Here you are, meditating on your body as a tree with a thousand lights, or as a spiderweb with a thousand strands: every point, every light, every strand connected to all other points. Your index finger alone represents 10 or 20 lights; your arm, another hundred or two hundred lights; the back, legs, and feet, another several hundred.
6. Vary the exercise: touch the wall with two or more fingers, touch it with both hands, touch it with a palm flat against the wall, with both palms flat, with fists. Now, while touching the wall with both palms flat, stay in the position for a while. It's as if you're doing a nearly vertical push-up, and you've stopped in mid-push. Is there a friend or colleague nearby? Ask them to come over and apply a little pressure to your back, for instance by pushing you a little with their own flat palms. Resist their pressure by using every point in your body, without overusing or underusing any point. Do you trust your friend and colleague not to hurt you? Ask them to increase the pressure little by little, so that you can increase your distributed resistance little by little.
7. You're learning to touch a surface (or object, person, musical instrument) with the whole of your body, in which a thousand points work together to give you distributed resistance. Apply the same general principle to holding a weight on your back or shoulders, to pushing an object (a pram, a piece of furniture, a heavy door), to holding an object, to applying pressure on an object (Figures 11.7, 11.8, and 11.9).

Rubber Bands

Gather ordinary rubber bands, like those that you have in the office or in the kitchen. Better still, go to the stationers' and buy a fresh supply, with rubber bands of many sizes and degrees of resistance.

The rubber band is an object with physical and material properties. At the same time, it's a rich and meaningful symbol, thanks to the interaction between the material properties and our imagination. In this exercise and meditation, we have two jobs: to develop technical skills employing the rubber bands, and to become alert to the symbolic dimension of the rubber bands. We'll intertwine the two jobs and their respective tasks.

What does the inner child do with a rubber band? In joy and in pleasure, the child plays with it as an object in itself rather than as a useful office implement. The child pulls on it, stretches, releases it; pulls some more, pulls too

Figure 11.7 Whole-body power. Credit: Anonymous via Pixabay.

Figure 11.8 Distributed effort. Credit: Hiep Hong.

STRENGTH REDEFINED

Figure 11.9 Whole-body poise. Credit: Jupi Lu.

much, breaks it. The child regrets breaking the toy but soon realizes that an inexhaustible supply of rubber bands is right there, at the child's disposal. Play becomes inexhaustible. You, the adult who is also the child, appreciate and celebrate inexhaustibility—a fine and big word for a fine and big idea.

The child resumes stretching and releasing the rubber band, and in a moment of inattention, the child releases the rubber band against her own hand. This hurts a little bit, but the child, surprised and startled, thinks that it hurts a lot. Tears ensue. You, the adult who is also the child, understand that the rubber band has a sort of power, like a weapon. You could hurt yourself, and you could hurt someone else. But you could also direct this power to launch something into space. The rubber band is a potential slingshot.

The child resumes stretching and releasing the rubber band. While holding it at a stretch, the child plucks it with a free finger. And the twang of the rubber band is the most marvelous thing in the whole world. You, the adult who is also the child, understand that the rubber band is a musical instrument, capable of pitch variation, dynamics, crescendo and diminuendo. The twang is very funny, and the rubber band transforms you into a clown and a trickster. And the twang is very pretty, and the rubber band transforms you into a sensitive musician from a land faraway (Figure 11.10).

The child resumes stretching and releasing the rubber band. The fingers are engaged; the fingers are awakened; the fingers want to play; the fingers

Figure 11.10 Rubber bands. Credit: StockSnap.

want to assert themselves. And you, the adult who is also the child, understand that you can combine fingers and rubber bands in dozens of different ways. Out of the inexhaustible box of rubber bands, you pick several, with different sizes and resistances, and you get different pairs of fingers to stretch under different types of rubber bands. The rubber band is a teacher of resistance, release, and ductility.

You, the adult who is also the child, love looking up words in the dictionary. Ductility is the ability of a material to sustain plastic deformation before it fractures. In your mind, the rubber band triggers an interesting insight about elasticity, and the next thing you know, you're testing sounds at the piano or the cello or the oboe to see how ductile your materials are, and how well you control your materials' ductility: the oboe reeds, the cello bow and strings, the piano keys and their connection to a whole edifice of hammers and springs.

The child resumes stretching and releasing the rubber band. And the child becomes ambitious and audacious, wrapping as many body parts as possible with one or more rubber bands: two fingers of the left hand, three of the right hand; a long rubber band hooking the crook of the thumb to the elbow; another long rubber band connecting one elbow to the other; a rubber band wrapped around the skull and jaw, like a hat strap. Every rubber band squeezes two or more body parts together, but the child resists the squeezes: if a rubber band pulls two fingers together, the child pulls the fingers apart; if a rubber band hooks the thumb to the elbow, the child attempts to increase the distance between the thumb and the elbow. You, the adult who is also the child, understand that the dialogue of opposing forces among all the rubber bands and all the body parts gives you a feeling of connectedness and strength. The rubber bands make for a strange straitjacket: friendly if you resist it, unfriendly if you yield to it.

The child resumes stretching and releasing the rubber band. But the contented child is worn out after so much excitement, and after a short time, she lovingly gathers all her rubber bands in a pouch and turns her attention to other toys, other tools. And you, the adult who is also the child, understand that you have integrated and internalized the rubber band: it now lives in your body and your mind as a set of memories, stories, and potentialities. You don't need an actual rubber band to manifest your own elasticity, resilience, and bounciness. Thanks to the rubber band, you've become a tensegrity structure.

Destroy a Newspaper

For this exercise, you need a newspaper. Its format and size don't matter, and its texts and images don't matter either. We'll be using it as an object usefully made of paper, rather than a source of news, gossip, or entertainment.

1. Handle the entire newspaper as if you've never seen a newspaper and you don't know what you're supposed to do with it. Hold it, lift it and drop it, caress it, smell it. The innocent and uninformed first approach helps you learn better and faster.
2. Sit at a table and put the newspaper down on the table. (And it doesn't matter if it's right side up or upside down; you won't read it anyway.) Now turn its pages, one by one or in twos and threes, slowly or quickly, carefully or sloppily. This is the page-turning exercise and meditation. If you like, put some music on in the background, for instance, a slow movement from a Mozart string quintet. Imagine that you're performing a solo show at a downtown theater. The quirky play or performance piece consists of your slowly turning the newspaper pages as music plays softly in the background. Or imagine that you've entered a monastery in Tibet, where the only meditation consists of your turning your newspaper pages, again and again, for several hours every day, for days and weeks and months until you reach gradual or sudden enlightenment. The newspaper as an object is now charged with ritualistic and performative potentialities, and your page-turning becomes hypnotic for you and for the people watching you (Figure 11.11).
3. The physicality of turning pages merits your attention. A newspaper page can be relatively large, and at the same time very light. The double

Figure 11.11 Newspaper. Credit: Victoria.

information (very large, very light) can be confusing or enlightening, depending on how you handle the page. Perhaps the newspaper is inciting you to be a big person with a delicate touch. We suspect that an accomplished dancer trained in South India will turn the newspaper differently from a distracted commuter on the subway, looking for the sports pages. Your job is to be the accomplished dancer sitting with perfect posture and turning the pages with a slow, deliberate, elegant, efficient gesture. This general attitude would serve you well when you play the piano, the cello, the piccolo, or any other musical instrument.

4. Turn a page, then turn it back. Turn a page using your dominant hand, turn a page using your nondominant hand. Turn a page with a quick gesture that produces a whooshing sound. The newspaper is your partner in a dance like no other. Turn a page looking at it intently; turn a page looking into the distance; turn a page with your eyes closed.

5. The next task is to take a page and crumple it, slowly or quickly, deliberately or agitatedly, and to crumple it into the smallest possible ball. It'll take determination and strength. After you achieve the Smallest Crumpled Paper Ball, throw it away without a second thought: on the floor in front of you, behind you, anywhere. Do this to a few pages: crumple, throw; crumple, throw. It can be a bit difficult for some people to throw anything, anywhere. If you grew up in a family where throwing is taboo, some part of you will shrink at the thought of throwing. If you're tidy and well-behaved, if you hate baseball, if you think that throwing is dirty or useless or inappropriate or ugly—well, there are many reasons why the act of throwing a crumpled ball of old newspaper would give you pause. Your hands, wrists, and fingers respond directly or indirectly to your taboos, your likes and dislikes, your judgments, your habits, everything that resides in your mind and heart. Throw you must, and throw in joy and pleasure you must. You'll clean up afterward and recycle the pages, and you'll be forgiven for your sins.

6. Crumple a page into the smallest, tightest ball imaginable. Don't throw it away. Instead, uncrumple it. You're sitting at the table; the tabletop is like an artist's working surface. Uncrumple and flatten the page, caressing it with your palms, applying some weight and pressure on the page. It's impossible to restore the page to its precrumpled state, but in your heart of hearts you'll do your utmost to heal the page from that cruel crumpling. Flatten, caress, flatten, caress; be the loving parent massaging the baby; be the disciplined artist flattening and caressing a page until the page thanks you for your dedication and attention.

7. The uncrumpled page is, I think, a beautiful and interesting object, like a 3D map showing elevations and other geographical features. No

Figure 11.12 After the crumpling. Credit: Anonymous via Pixabay.

two uncrumpled pages could ever be exactly alike. The uncrumpled page, then, is a symbol of uniqueness. And it also stands as a sort of self-portrait: you crumpled it, you uncrumpled it; no one else would have achieved your elevations, your geographical features. Your hands, wrists, and fingers are forever drawing your self-portrait. It's useful to notice the phenomenon and enjoy its manifestations (Figure 11.12).

8. For the next exercise, you can use an uncrumpled page or a fresh one that has never been crumpled in its life. Your job is to tear the page to shreds. This, too, is an art with many subtle variations. Start by tearing a single strip from a page; tear a vertical strip, then tear a horizontal one. You'll discover an amazing fact: because of its fibers, the paper tears very differently according to the direction of the tear. One direction is smooth and easy to control, allowing you to produce a steady rip that creates a symmetrical strip. The other direction is jagged and difficult to control; you'll struggle to tear a tidy strip. Strip as you would a Band-Aid off a hairy spot: carefully, hair by hair; or in one sudden fast gesture.

9. The materiality of the newspaper instructs your arms, hands, wrists, and fingers—but also your whole back, head, neck, and shoulders. The texture of the paper, its size and weight, and its behavior under your touch make it like playing a strange instrument, which in its very strangeness invites you to become more alert to yourself.

10. For the last task, make a paper airplane using your nondominant hand only. The strange or counterintuitive action gets you to see yourself in a new light. It's not obligatory to produce an aerodynamic object; it's recommended to have a good time.

Pillow Kneading

Go get a pillow somewhere in your house. It helps if the pillow is nicely dimensioned, clean, and in good shape. But any pillow will do.

1. As always in our method, start by playing with the pillow without a preconceived plan. Caress its surface, squeeze it a little, bring it up against your head, and sense its textures. The familiar object offers you a lot of information, including many pleasures and many stories.
2. Lay the pillow down on an easy-to-reach surface, perhaps a table. Or sit comfortably and put the pillow on your lap. Don't start kneading it just yet. Instead, run one or both hands along the surface of the pillow, sensing the texture of its covering, which is like a skin, and the knobs and bumps in the pillow's inside, its body. Perhaps the pillow has no knobs and bumps; your light and sensitive touch will inform you either way.
3. It's useful to imagine that you must describe the pillow to someone who can't see it, or that you'll draw or paint the pillow after spending time with it. This makes you more attentive.
4. With one or both hands, caress the pillow's surface, then start increasing the pressure of your hands. The average pillow yields to your pressure and resists it at the same time. Feathers, down, memory foam, microbeads: different pillows, different types of yielding and resisting. The pillow embodies qualities present in many other objects and surfaces, in the human body, in cats and dogs and other animals; and, more indirectly and subtly, in musical instruments. A cello string resists and yields to pressure, much as a pillow does; the membranes on timpani aren't completely different from pillows in this respect.
5. Knead the pillow with both hands. How can you vary your touch, and in how many gradations? Caress, squeeze, twist, press, clasp, enfold, pinch, slap, punch. We imagine that the pillow is a sentient being, a pet, a friend; and we imagine that the pillow welcomes our kneading and feels good when we squeeze it. We imagine that the pillow has a core, a central point. We imagine that we want to find that point with our kneading and make the pillow purr when we get there. Creative Health is a widening of possibilities, the exploration

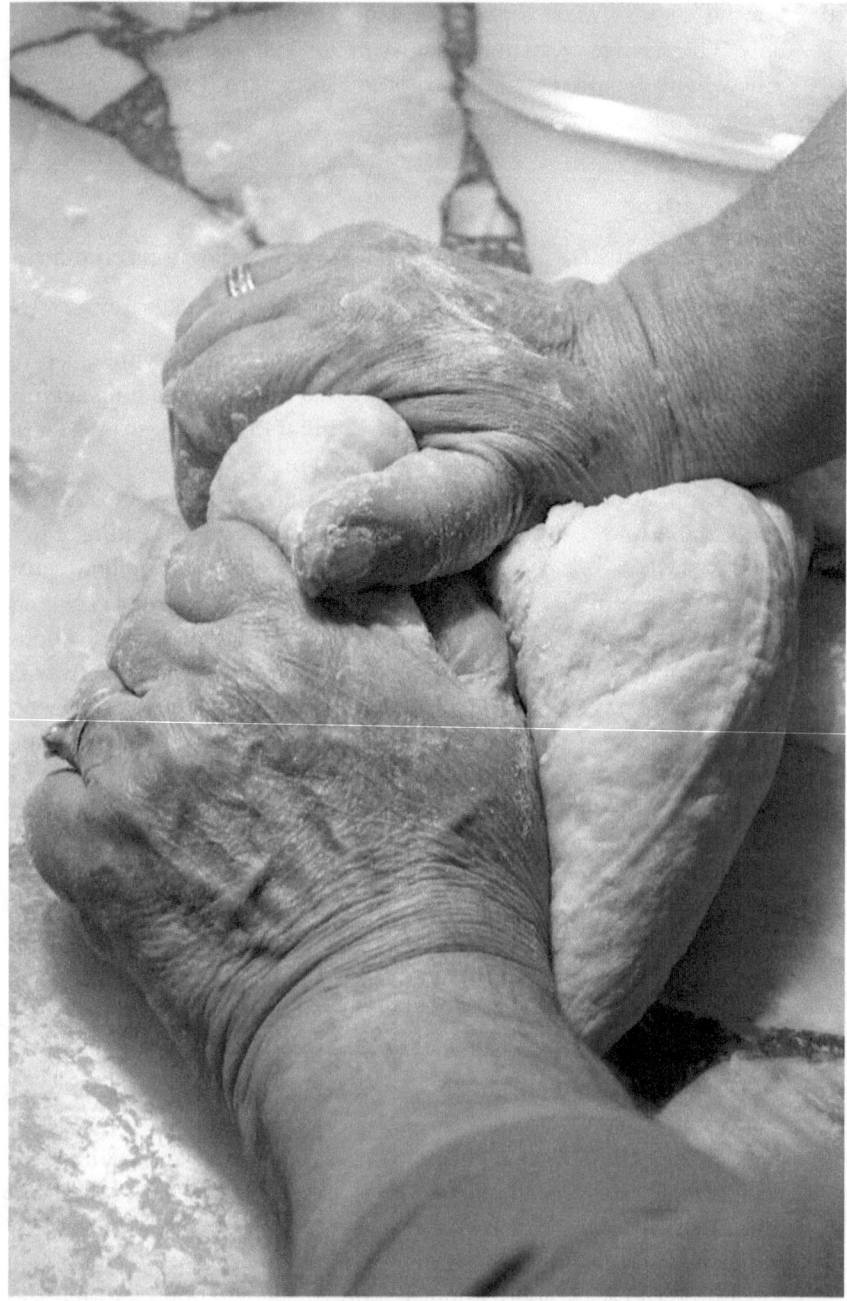

Figure 11.13 Kneading. Credit: Anonymous via Pixabay.

of ever greater variety, the pushing of boundaries. Creative Health doesn't exclude willful hallucinations and unconstrained head trips. Creative Health talks to pillows and listens to the pillows when they talk back at us. Creative Health is a paradox: a silly game and serious business.

6. Kneading is more demanding than it appears at first. Do your hands start hurting after you knead the pillow for a while? Slow down. Lighten your touch. Stop kneading, and let your hands rest quietly on top of the pillow. The development of strength and endurance is a long-term project, and it requires an adaptable rhythm of effort and rest.

Newspapers, rubber bands, pillows; piano keys, cello strings, embouchures; head, neck, back, shoulders, pelvis, legs; hands, wrists, fingers: let there be a harmony of tensions, and Creative Health will flourish (Figure 11.13).

Chapter 12

REPETITIVE PRACTICE

Repetition is the foundation of life.

Breathing is a repetitive act that you perform thousands of times every day. Walking is repetitive, too, whether you walk down the block to the bakery or take ten thousand steps as a meditative exercise. You might not notice how many times you chew a mouthful of peanuts, but it's unlikely that you chew only once or twice before swallowing the 20 crunchy things. Kissing your lover is also repetitive. Depending on who you are, you might give and receive a hundred kisses before you feel the urge to check the messages on your smartphone. Checking messages also happens to be a repetitive action. Sports, martial arts, dance: repetitive. Peeling potatoes, carrots, beets: repetitive. Singing, speaking, chanting: repetitive.

Let me repeat it: repetition is the foundation of life.

And if repetition is foundational, so is repetitive practice for musicians. Repetition helps you learn, internalize, remember, and integrate your musical gestures and texts. Repetition helps you become attentive and discerning. Repetition brings you joy and pleasure. Repetition can also hurt you and disrupt your music making, perhaps even your career and livelihood.

Five concepts will help you practice repetitions for 10 minutes, 60 minutes, or three hours without hurting yourself. Each of these concepts requires intentionality and awareness.

1. Make choices and decisions.
2. Organize your whole self.
3. Explore gradations.
4. Employ the energies of the actor, the receptor, and the witness.
5. Connect with the linguistic impulse.

Make Choices and Decisions

Our lives are made of a string of choices and decisions. Some of them are banal: "Do I set up the alarm clock for 6:45 AM or for 7 AM?" Others are more impactful: "Do I accept the job offer from the symphony orchestra, or do I continue my career as a freelancer?" Whether the choices are banal or important, the main thing is to realize that to live is to make choices. To practice, then, is to make choices; and to practice repetitively is to make many choices quickly, one after the other. Repetitive practice helps you become a skillful decision-maker.

Is the repetitive gesture hurting you? You can choose to stop and take a break, to stop altogether, to push through the pain, to tweak your playing in some way, to move on to a different exercise. Are you getting bored, annoyed, angry? It happens to all of us. And we all can choose to stop or to go on, to laugh at our own anger, or to get angry at our own anger. Lower your shoulder, raise your elbow, rotate your arm, relax your thumb, sit straight, cross your legs, uncross your legs, play faster, play more slowly. Psychological decisions, physical decisions, technical decisions, musical decisions, one after the other, many decisions taken at the same time: repetitive practice is an art form in and of itself.

Repetitive practice is like walking through an intricate neighborhood in a city, foreign or familiar. Are you going from point A to point B, or will you go to point C instead? Which monuments will you visit, which will you skip? Where do you want to linger, and for how long? Will you turn left or right, will you continue straight on, will you turn around and backtrack? No two visits need be exactly alike (Figure 12.1).

Organize Your Whole Self

Your hands, wrists, and fingers are supremely important. The challenge is to balance the attention you give them with the attention you give to everything else involved in music making. Among other aspects, the long list includes ergonomics (chairs, stools, music stands, light, ventilation, heat and cold, humidity, the acoustics of the room where you find yourself); the coordination of the whole body from head to toe; your general frame of mind (alert or not, patient or not, joyful or not); and your relationship to music itself. Repetitive practice requires that you keep track of all these dimensions at the same time. If you concentrate on hands, wrists, and fingers and exclude head, neck, and back from your awareness, you're courting trouble; if you ignore ergonomics, you're courting trouble; if you're irritated and annoyed, you're courting trouble; if you don't know your time signatures and your sharps and flats, you're courting trouble.

Coordination isn't a matter of physical relaxation but psychophysical organization, which depends on a dialogue of latent resistance and latent mobility. Imagine that your body consists of a thousand points, evenly distributed. Every point has its capacity to be firm and still; every point has its capacity to yield to pressure or to move in space. And those thousand points

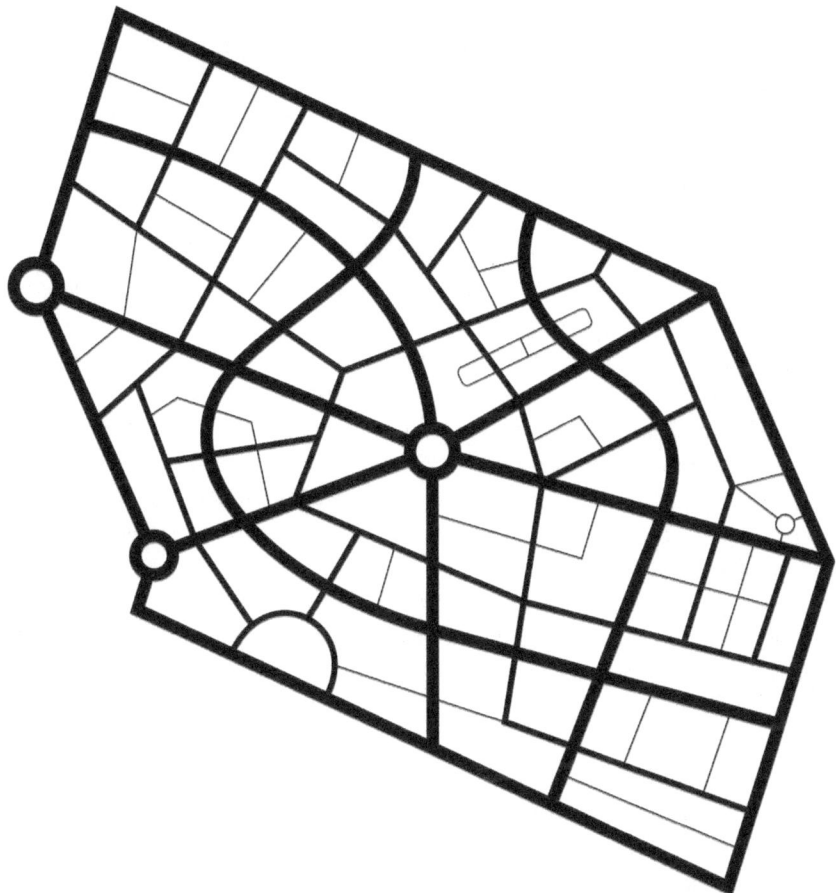

Figure 12.1 A grid of choices. Credit: χρίς.

have a thousand friends in your attentive mind. I know this is somewhat abstract, so I'll say it differently:

Attention, stillness, movement;
attention, stillness, movement.

Attention, stillness, movement;
attention, stillness, movement.

Explore Gradations

How many grains of salt does the perfect cookie require? There are two types of cookie eaters: the ones for whom the amount of salt must be ideally measured against the amount of butter and chocolate, and the ones for whom what matters most is to put that cookie in their mouth and eat it, *now*! Let's aim for something both impossible and useless: the capacity for your fingertips to tell the difference between one grain of salt and two grains of salt. Failing that, let's aim to make our hands and fingers ever more sensitive, to the extent that we can.

Suppose that you need to unlock a door you're unfamiliar with. The key must fit in a certain way, with a little bit of give, and you can't turn the key too quickly or the lock will refuse your touch. Without sensitivity to gradations, you won't be able to open that door.

The healthy hands, wrists, and fingers are sensitive to gradations of all sorts: gradations of pressure, strength, distribution of muscle tension, heat, and cold; gradations of resistance, for instance on the skin of a tomato as you slice it thin for a carpaccio, or the resistance of a violin string as you play it; gradations of distance as you travel up and down the fingerboard, comma by comma, quarter tone by quarter tone, or up and down the keyboard, semitone by semitone.

Repetitive practice is a perfect territory for the exploration of gradations. Choose a task that isn't difficult to perform, freeing you from technical and psychological worries. For example, decide that you'll play the first five notes of a major scale, at a steady moderate speed, up and down, up and down. How many gradations of dynamics do you have at your disposal? How many types of articulations for each note? How many gradations of speed? Play the few notes of the exercise, then take your inner metronome up by a single tick and play again. Tick by tick, slowly accelerate the exercise. You'll soon see that you can play any one thing 50 times in a row without ever repeating the same exact gesture (Figures 12.2 and 12.3).

Actor, Receptor, Witness

Living and working inside you, three distinct forces shape your experiences: the actor, the receptor, and the witness. The actor is a doer, making decisions and carrying them out as actions in the physical and material world. The receptor is like a sensitive membrane, endlessly responding to each situation with a wealth of sensations, feelings, and emotions. Sounds, textures, tastes, temperatures, movements, postures, pleasures, and displeasures are the domain of the receptor. And the witness observes and analyzes things, situations, people, and actions without passing judgment. The witness doesn't get emotionally involved; it simply takes in the facts, describes the goal or the task or situation, and synthesizes information.

REPETITIVE PRACTICE 169

Figure 12.2 Varied gradations. Credit: Marijana.

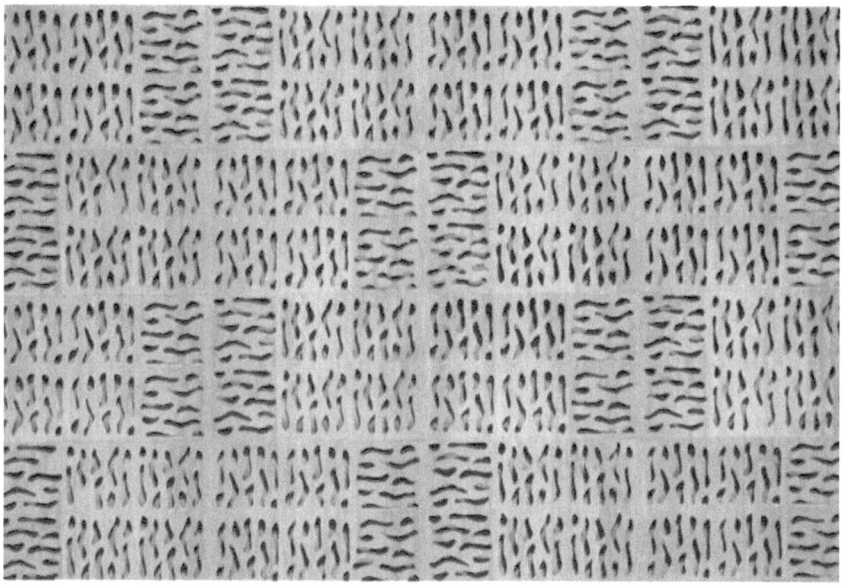

Figure 12.3 Organized gradations. Credit: Franck Barske.

The challenge is getting these dimensions or energies to work together in harmony. The actor may become fixated on doing, pushing for more, faster, harder, never stopping. Walking down the corridors of a music school, you can hear fixated young doers playing ceaselessly, sometimes making and repeating the same mistakes dozens of times. The receptor sometimes becomes overwhelmed by too many emotions and sensations, and we know how harmful sensory overload can be. And the witness, analyzing every detail and listing every possible danger inherent in a situation, can inhibit action altogether. The invasive witness in charge of everything doesn't let the little kid dip a toe in a shallow swimming pool.

Repetitive practice becomes the space where the three forces engage in a continuous dialogue. Imagine that you're playing the same four-bar phrase twelve times in a row. The actor makes decisions and initiates every gesture. If you're playing right now, it's because the actor in you determined that you were going to play. The receptor captures sensations of sound and movement, feeling the pressure of the bow on the string, the pressure of the breath passing through the oboe reeds, the transfer of arm, hand, and finger weight onto the piano keyboard. And the witness provides an objective overview, keeping track of the initial task and analyzing how things are going relative to the chosen task.

Responding with enjoyment or discomfort, the receptor tends to pass judgment: "Wonderful, crappy, I like it, I dislike it, I love it, I hate it, I'm good, I'm not good." The receptor can be a perfectionist, a narcissist, a divo or a diva swimming or drowning in emotions and sensations. Let's suppose that the receptor abhors a certain sound that you've just made. The actor, in response, pushes harder, trying to improve the sound but creating errors instead. It's only when you step back and let the witness speak that you can break the cycle of overdoing and overjudging. "I rushed the downbeat of the third bar. In the second bar, the triplets and their chromatics distracted me from the continuity of intention and gesture." Then the actor has a new and different goal, which isn't to just do it again and again, but to understand the sharps and double sharps in the second bar and to provide continuity from bar to bar. The receptor tunes in and monitors the intervals, the articulations, the pressures, the sensorial results of the gestures that the actor and the witness proposed that you make (Figure 12.4).

The Linguistic Impulse

Repetitive practice takes its life and flow from a mix of technical decisions and linguistic choices. Suppose that you're playing an open string on the violin. Dozens of parameters merit your attention: the point of contact of the

Figure 12.4 Relaxed focus. Credit: Jiradet Inrungruan.

bow on the string, the tilt of the bow, your overall posture, the height of your elbow, and so on. The musical drone of the steady open string is a meditation on sound, harmonics, timbre, and volume. You're saying, singing, and chanting something meaningful and timeless. Ultimately, your technical decisions and your linguistic choices are one and the same.

Most of the music that we play is linguistically organized. Take the four-bar phrase as an example. It's impossible to play Franz Schubert, the blues, folk music, marches, and church hymns without encountering four-bar phrases by the dozens and hundreds. In the blues, the four-bar phrases are stated in groups of three for a total of twelve bars. In other contexts, four-bar phrases come in twos and fours. Sing Beethoven's "Ode to Joy" (from the Ninth Symphony), and you'll sing four-bar phrases four times in a row. Each couple of phrases makes for a question-and-answer structure: question, answer; second question, final answer. Repetitive practice works best when every gesture, every note, every scale, every phrase, every breath, every crescendo, and every diminuendo is born of your linguistic commitment.

Repetition is the foundation of life.

Three Meditations Not About Drawing

Drawing can be seen as a specialized artistic skill or as a natural, informal, and nonspecialized gesture—like the countless times we've doodled during a dull lecture. Here I'm not asking you to become a devoted art student aiming to draw well. Instead, I'm inviting you to use a few drawing exercises to infuse your hands, wrists, and fingers with lively intentionality. Let's not call it drawing, but playing the Graphitone, that marvelous instrument from our inner Wonderland.

You only need a few sheets of paper and a pencil. If you're artistically inclined, you may of course use fine papers of many types, soft pencils, hard pencils, anything you want.

1. Sit at a table with paper and pencil ready in front of you. With your hands, lightly touch your skull, forehead, jaw, and sternum. Sit upright without looking at the paper, pick up your pencil, and draw a short line. Put the pencil down and start again: skull, forehead, jaw, sternum; without looking at the paper, draw another line. This trains your hands to become secondary to your commitment to poise and good posture.
2. The exercise is harder than it seems. You won't want to stay upright. You won't want to tap your skull, forehead, jaw, and sternum. You won't want to not look at the paper. Little monkeys will invade your mind, distracting and annoying you. You'll be tempted to blame the exercise itself, not your monkey mind.
3. How many times will you repeat the procedure? How many lines will you draw? For how long will you persevere? You choose. How will you deal with the monkeys? You choose.

4. "Do the lines have to be straight, symmetrical, and pretty?" That's a monkey-mind type of question. The lines arise by themselves, because of your overall state of mind and body. Posture and intentionality create lines of a certain type; agitation and distraction create lines of another type.
5. "Why drawing? Why can't I do a similar exercise with my instrument? Why can't I sit at the piano and do the skull-jaw thing and play a note or ten? I hate drawing." Your monkey mind is talking again. You can do anything you want. It's wonderful to do the exercise at the piano or the guitar or any other instrument. And who said anything about drawing? You're practicing the Graphitone. You're learning John Cage's "Graphitone Tarantella," which he discomposed especially for you.
6. Creative Health is a wonderful game. Mastery of the game—no, that's the start of a monkey mind statement. Mastery doesn't play a role in this game (Figure 12.5).

Here's the second non-drawing drawing exercise.

1. Draw a small, closed geometric shape of your choosing: square, circle, triangle, diamond. Now fill the entire shape with pencil. One monkey tells you to cover the circle perfectly, or else! Another monkey will tell you to be careless on purpose because it's a stupid game and a waste of your time, plus you hate drawing. If you could only watch a video of you filling the circle, you'd be amazed at the little monkeys flying all around you, squeaking and squawking.
2. You probably know some musicians who play their instruments while a swarm of squeaking monkeys flies all around them. The monkeys aren't just in their minds, but in their sounds, their interpretations, their bodily movements, their hands, wrists, and fingers. And I'm not saying that you play this way yourself. I'm just saying.
3. Maybe the skull-jaw thing of the previous exercise would be helpful.
4. Draw a bigger closed shape, geometric or not, and fill it in. Decades ago, I met the late Patrick Heron, an accomplished painter of mostly abstract compositions. Some of his paintings were huge. He liked using a fine Japanese brush to cover the canvas with delicate, continuous touches of paint. He wanted the painted surfaces not to show any discontinuity in the form of uneven brush strokes. Sometimes he painted for nine hours without a break to avoid cutoff lines.
5. In sports and exercise, cross-training has long been advocated as a way of increasing flexibility, resistance, and strength. By cross-training, you engage more muscle groups and more functions of your mind than you

Figure 12.5 Monkey mind. Credit: sharkolot.

would by practicing a single sport. A basketball player who spends time playing baseball and golf might become a more complete basketball player. A musician who spends time drawing might become a more complete musician.

Here's the third non-drawing drawing exercise.

1. Cover an entire sheet of paper with pencil. It won't take nine hours; it won't take nine innings.
2. Erase the pencil marks slowly, caressing the paper with the eraser at a slow tempo. Remember the skull-jaw thing, also called posture and intentionality. Listen to music as you caress the paper. Or sing to yourself, talk to yourself, talk to a friend who's doing the exercise with you
3. If the monkey tells you that you aren't a visual artist but a musician, think of the great composers laboring long hours with pen and staff paper. Think of Franz Schubert's gigantic output over just a few years and how much time he must have spent writing music by hand. Think of Igor Stravinsky writing down "Le Sacre du Printemps," absolutely determined to produce a beautiful score that was an artwork in and of itself. Every composer is a graphic designer, every composer is a calligrapher; all composers skillfully use their hands, wrists, and fingers away from their beloved instruments.

Repetition is the foundation of life.

One Hundred Beans

For this exercise you need a cupful of dry beans, red, black, brown, white; it probably doesn't matter. A mixture of colors would stimulate the eyes and the imagination. If you're a homework fanatic, get more than a cup—a kilo, for instance. And get a bowl as well. If you have a beautiful ceramic bowl, that would be nice. But a metal bowl has its merits, too, its sounds, its histories and traditions.

I'm describing the exercise informally, with relatively messy instructions. I'm doing it on purpose, addressing your right brain, your head-tripping imagination, your intuition, your curiosity, your sensorial mind. Your analytical mind may find this process vague, incomplete, wasteful, and repetitive. But the very spirit of repetitive practice welcomes repetition. I'll repeat and vary the instructions a dozen times, maybe more.

Repetition is the foundation of life! (Figure 12.6)

Figure 12.6 Beans, one by one. Credit: Daniel Ramirez.

A cup of dry beans plus a bowl. Your job is simple: empty the cup of beans on a tabletop. Now place the beans in the bowl. Count the beans out loud as you put them in the bowl: one, two, three, four … The official minimum for the exercise is one hundred beans, counted out loud, and placed in the bowl one by one, without hurry or impatience, in good cheer. If it takes you four seconds per bean, it only takes four hundred seconds to count a hundred beans. It's under seven minutes; it's less than a symphony movement. If you were to count beans for the duration of Wagner's "Tetralogy," you'd need about 64,800 beans, probably some 25 kilos. Not practical, but not impossible either.

I went from the straightforward left brain (a cup of dry beans plus a bowl) to the imaginative right brain (Wagner, 64,800 beans, the ride of the Valkyries, the golden ring, family dynamics, horrible deaths). I'm doing this on purpose; I'm trying to get you to sense your hands through a dialogue of left and right brain, the straightforward and mechanical intertwined with the labyrinthine and unpredictable. It's how your hands work and live, and you might as well be with them in their natural habitat.

With your delicate fingers, pick a bean off the table, lift it, drop it in the bowl. Pick, lift, drop. A hundred beans aren't that many at all. And four seconds per bean is a bit too short. What if you want to push the bean here and there a little before picking it up? What if you want to caress the bean before lifting it? What if you want to look at the bean closely, and notice how elegant it is, how shiny, how beautiful? What if you want to address the bean for a moment, say hi, give it a compliment, then say goodbye as you drop the bean onto the bowl?

It'd take longer. But you'd be training your fingers to be attentive and delicate, and you'd be training your brain to be attentive and delicate. You'd be practicing the art of making gestures plus the art of Object Wisdom. You'd keep track of beans and numbers. Do you know how upsetting it is to suddenly realize that in your counting you jumped from 75 to 77? You'd have to start all over again.

One hundred beans lying on the table; a bowl; pick a bean, lift it, drop it. That's the exercise (Figure 12.7).

The ostensible exercise, according to the left brain, is simple, repetitive, senseless, boring, annoying, and useless. The real exercise, according to the right brain, is a meditation on time, commitment, and attention; a deep practice of delicate skills that make your fingers astute and precise; a fairytale in which you are the aggrieved stepdaughter of the wicked second wife, who has commanded you to do an impossible task as a way to demean you and prove to you and to your hapless father that you're worthless and should be confined to the basement, if not purged from the household altogether. As you perform the assigned task by yourself in the dark kitchen, a friendly mouse comes to

Figure 12.7 A collection of beans. Credit: Gideon Putra.

your aid and rewards your good heart with magical gifts. The wicked stepmother meets a grisly end.

One hundred beans; pick, lift, drop. Count out loud: one, two, three, four … Keep track of the beans and the numbers. Listen to each bean as it lands in the bowl. The left brain calls it torture; delighting in the subtle music, the right brain goes off on a trip in space and time: Tibet, Zen temples in Kyoto, raindrops keep fallin' on my head (Figure 12.8).

One hundred beans. If you stay with the exercise, the repetitiveness helps you organize your gestures. Brain, fingers, and counting start to sync. Neurology probably has things to say about it, and probably calls those things "dopamine."

It's useful to recognize how many repetitive practices there are in your daily life and in your music life. If you make a big vat of carrot soup, you might peel 20 carrots, at about 10 peeling motions per carrot: two hundred swishes of the peeler. Cooking is generally repetitive, and often meditative. Addressing envelopes by hand for a wedding: two hundred envelopes, eight hundred lines of names, streets, numbers, postal codes. Painting a wall in your living room: priming it, first coat, second coat; repetitive, meditative. The list is very long. You might want to interrupt me and tell me that you hate peeling carrots and writing by hand. I won't disagree with you, but instead, I might try to persuade you to embrace the task, alter your timing, find rhythm

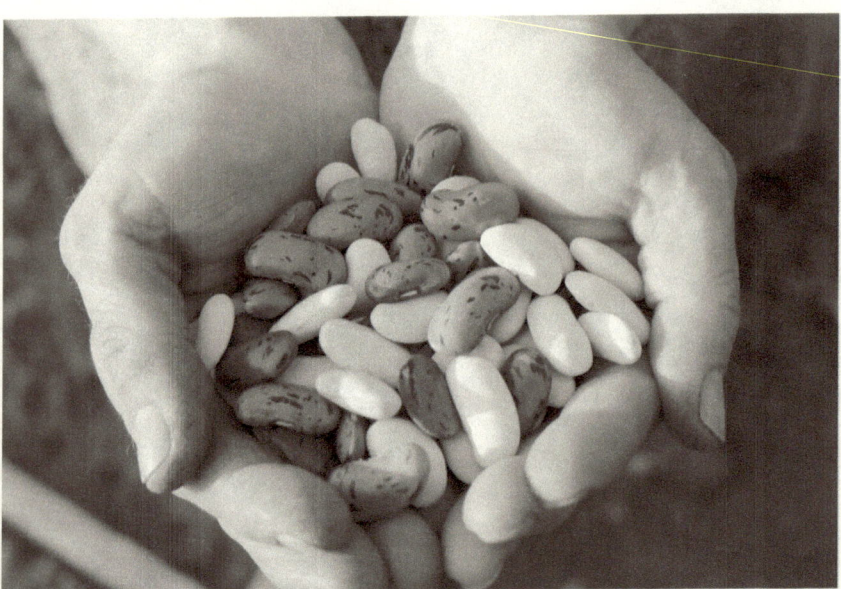

Figure 12.8 Varied beans. Credit: Pexels.

and flow, and change your attitude from hatred to acceptance and, if possible, to love.

One hundred beans. It's not that many. It'll take a couple of minutes. Count them out loud as you place them in a bowl, one by one. Use a metronome. I still have an old analog metronome from my years as a student. Thanks to it, I can set up a beat, one or more subdivisions, and a time signature. I know you can do the same with a digital metronome, including the one on your smartphone. But to have a sort of historical object in your hands, something with a personality, with many stories to tell ... it's incomparable. My metronome is a Boss Dr. Beat, model DB-33. Its ticking is so pretty that my digital metronome has a "Dr. Beat" sound setting. The metronome is my friend, my companion, my collaborator; it's steady and reliable, unlike some of my own beats; the metronome is a mirror, showing me who I am and where I'm at, metrically. I regret not using my metronome more frequently, and not having used it more in the past (Figure 12.9).

One, two, three ... four, five, six ... bean by bean to a steady beat. Insert metronomically timed silences between groups of beans. Structure the counting as a phrase and string your phrases in a sequence like a composition.

Joseph Haydn's Symphony No. 101 in D major, premiered in London in 1794, is popularly known as "The Clock" on account of a ticktock effect in the second movement. This is only one example of a composition with a

Figure 12.9 Collected beans. Credit: sandrinessouza.

repetitive and hypnotic pattern that brings joy to an audience. Your bean counting may be less elaborate than Haydn's music, but it's a manifestation of the same principle and offers similar pleasures: the metronome as heartbeat and reassurance, the metronome as an organizing factor, the metronome as helper and friend.

If not a metronome, then put some "actual music" on. I use quotation marks because I consider a metronome's beat as actual music, too—extremely streamlined and yet vital, a germinating seed, the DNA of certain types of compositions. Anyway, put some music on and go back to your beans. The music can have a steady beat which you follow with your gestures, or it can be nonmetric like Gregorian chant. And even if the music in the background does have a steady beat, you could choose to ignore its beat and let the music do its thing while you do yours.

A cup of beans, a bowl; transfer the beans from the cup to the bowl, one by one; or spill the cup of beans out on the table or the countertop and pick each bean in turn and deposit it in the bowl. Count the beans out loud. Use a metronome, or not; play music in the background, or not. Enjoy it, or not. You make choices and decisions. You organize your whole self from head and neck to feet and toes. You let the actor, the receptor, and the witness play the game with you. You vary gradations of speed and gesture. And you hew to a linguistic principle, here manifested as counting.

Repetition is the foundation of life.

Musician at Work

The possibilities are endless.

1. Every gesture lends itself to repetition, including those that don't involve sounds: for instance, opening and closing your instrument case; lifting your instrument to playing position, then bringing it back down; walking toward a music stand, walking away from it.
2. A single note embodies Music. It merits being repeated *ad aeternum*. Imagine a ceremony where you, the herald of beauty, sound the one note for the elevation of the audience. It doesn't matter if you play the tin whistle or the trombone; temporarily you're now playing the shofar at a synagogue. You're expected to blow the shofar one hundred times during the service, using a combination of long and short sounds. Let your repetitive practice be a timeless call.
3. The root of the word "two" is related to the root of the word "doubt." "One" signifies wholeness, indivisibility, certainty; "two" shows that something has been divided and isn't so certain anymore. Play a note:

it symbolizes wholeness. Play two notes: they symbolize division. Two notes in sequence merit repeated practice until your heart grasps the very meaning of wholeness, division, and restoration of wholeness.
4. Fingers articulating a note on the flute or the trumpet, without you blowing into the instrument and making sounds: they merit repeated practice. A single chord at the piano, with your body and mind working on the required weight transfer from the back to the arms to the

Figure 12.10 Reliable repetition. Credit: Pete Linforth.

Figure 12.11 Built-in repetition. Credit: Taken.

keyboard: it merits repeated practice. The first four notes of a well-known sonata or concerto; four self-contained measures; two sets of four measures, articulating a question and an answer: every imaginable musical event merits repeated practice.

5. Pick a four-minute piece in your repertory. Whether vocal or instrumental, it's constructed of syllables, words, phrases, and paragraphs. Repeat each syllable endlessly. Repeat a syllable three or four times, then follow it with the next syllable in the word. Repeat a word of two or three syllables—that is, two or three notes that belong together. Repeat a phrase—that is, four bars containing multiple words of two, three, four, or five sounds each. Repeat a paragraph—that is, two sets of four-bar phrases. Building up the four-minute piece through repeated practice of its component parts might take you 20 minutes or more.

Repetition is the foundation of life (Figures 12.10 and 12.11).

Part IV
KNOWLEDGE AND MYSTERY

Figure IV Connection. Credit: Olcay ertem.

Chapter 13

ENERGY

How many handshakes have you given and received in your life? Thousands if you count specific individuals, tens of thousands if you count all handshakes.

You've sensed hands both hot and cold, tight and loose, reassuring and aggressive, invested and indifferent. A certain handshake brings on a clear message: "This is a very masculine energy." Another handshake triggers a different thought: "Feminine energy. Strange, I didn't expect it from this particular person." Oftentimes the handshake suggests images, metaphors, stories: "Ouch, he's just like a used-car salesman in a B movie." "Osteopath for rugby players, or something. I could get into it." "She thinks I'm cookie dough. If this goes on for another minute, she'll try to bake me." "Friend." "Enemy" (Figure 13.1).

Over the years you played for many types of conductors, or you watched them in action. Some have jagged movements with sharp corners, like a Cubist painting in motion. Others evoke military drills, strict disciplinarians, robots. Others still have the shakes: arms, hands, fingers, hair, shoulders, convulsions, a tornado, an earthquake. The convulsive conductor might produce great results from the orchestra, or not; the Cubist, maybe or maybe not; the drill sergeant, maybe or maybe not. The main thing is for us to note that there are many, many types of conducting styles.

Handshakes are a dialogue of energies. Conductors are fountains of propagating energy. Every person you meet gives off energy. Whether you're alert to it or not, you too give and receive energy all day long. To play one note is to direct and propagate your energy.

We won't attempt to define energy. Instead, we'll practice the art of sensing and directing our own varied and vital energies.

In Praise of Make-Believe and Playacting

Watch children at a playground. They teach themselves games and skills of many types: how to interact with other children and with adults, how to get attention and how to evade attention, how to climb up and down a rope

Figure 13.1 Energy of touch. Credit: Heung Soon.

sculpture, how to dribble, how to attack, how to defend. Before they can speak, babies and toddlers play conversation. My siblings and I used to play Funeral. I liked being the corpse or the priest better than being a mourner. Children play Doctor, and what they learn isn't necessarily medicine. To live is to play and learn. Imitation teaches you wonders. Pretending accelerates understanding and integration. Making a fool of yourself on purpose is fantastically liberating.

For some adults, the reflex of play is alive and well. For others, it's more latent than active. And some adults really dislike the notion of playing to learn, and really, really hate even the faint possibility of making a fool of themselves. Here I'm inviting all my readers, the enthusiastic and the doubtful, the foolish and the wise, to play and to give reign to their imagination.

Years ago, I gave a talk to a group of about thirty people. With the help of a woman volunteer, I demonstrated an exercise that helps you sense and direct the energies circulating around your head. A man in the audience raised his hand. "I'm an engineer, and I know that those energies that you're talking about don't exist." After the talk ended, I went to chat with the engineer. He again expressed his disappointment with my work, but then he changed his tone of voice and said something else. "Whatever you showed that woman, it seemed to help her." A lightbulb brightened my mind, and I thought to myself: "The *intellectual placebo*—a patently false idea that actually works." I didn't tell the engineer that he had just helped me invent a useful concept, but I'll never forget him.

Let's suppose that you find these general ideas of energy vague or objectionable. Play the game, even if you do it halfheartedly or in a spirit of mockery. The intellectual placebo might still work its magic on you.

Hands

Sitting or standing, bring your palms close to each other without touching, fingers neither floppy nor stiff. Rotate your hands at a moderate speed in semicircles, varying their distance, height, and speed. Let's say you're holding an invisible grapefruit and slowly rotating it back and forth with your hands. You might sense warmth, pressure, elasticity, or something resembling a magnetic charge. It's possible that you'll sense nothing to begin with; be patient and persevere. And if you feel nothing now or ever in the future, stay with the exercise for the sake of staying with the exercise.

The space between your hands is pliable. Pull, stretch, and shape the space; move your hands farther apart, then again closer together in a slow and flexible dance. We tend to assign clear boundaries between our bodies and space: my body ends *here*, and from here on the empty space starts. This exercise might trigger the sensation that your body and the space outside your body are less clearly separated than you used to think. The boundary softens, and the energy of your hands melds with the energy of the space around the hands.

Pointing

Pointing is an amazingly powerful endeavor. Pointing is naming and numbering, choosing and focusing. Pointing selects, isolates, and elevates the thing being pointed, making it important to the person doing the pointing: "That one over there; not this one, *that* one." The power of pointing is acknowledged when we discourage it: "Pointing is rude." In some settings, to point at someone is to accuse the person in question, and perhaps condemn him or her to death. There are cultures in which pointing is considered to bring bad luck to the person being pointed at. And in some cultures, it's taboo to point at a sacred object or a person in a position of authority (Figures 13.2 and 13.3).

We won't play with life and death. Instead, we'll use pointing as a tool to energize our minds, our eyes, our arms, our hands, wrists, and fingers.

You don't point with your finger, but with your person. Someone quickly hails a taxi with a well-directed arm, energized with intention; someone else, hesitant and timid, waits forever by the sidewalk, invisible to the passing cabs.

Figure 13.2 Energy of pointing. Credit: Rapheal Nathaniel.

Figure 13.3 Speaking and pointing. Credit: Rob Slaven.

Organize your whole self from head to toe, lengthening and widening your back, rooting your shoulder blade in your wide back. Stretch an arm with pleasure and authority. Extend an index finger as if into infinity.

1. Go around your house, pointing at features in the rooms: window; windowpane; third windowpane down from the top, on the left.
2. Stand by a bookshelf and point at each book in turn; read its title out loud, and the pointing also becomes a naming.
3. You can be close to something and point at it, or you can be far removed from it and point at it. Pointing can telescope in and out. It's not simply a matter of stretching or shrinking your arm, but of expanding your attention and your imagination.
4. Stand by a window somewhere inside your home, then point at things across the street: neighbors' windows, a passing car, clouds.
5. You can point at a fixed object or at a moving object. Pointing, too, becomes fixed or mobile.
6. Find a map and point at countries, then at cities. Let your fingertip touch the map, and pointing is now physically intimate.
7. If you are a pianist or if you have a piano or other keyboard available to you, point at a key and name it: "Middle C. B flat below middle C." I know that you know the keys and their names, but when you embrace pointing as a discipline of energy propagation, the familiar keys take on a sort of urgency and they start shining in your imagination.
8. Point at something—a poster or painting in your room, or a tree across the street. Point firmly, with the desire to reach the thing in question. Look at the thing and point at it. Pointing without looking has its own merit, but here you're looking and pointing, with intention and desire. Point and look, and sustain the gesture for a good while, let's say 30 seconds. It's quite a long time if you aren't used to it.
9. Point with your index finger; point with the dominant hand; point with the nondominant hand.
10. Point with determination. Point with joy. Point with resentment or anger. Point and believe, believe, believe!
11. Point briefly, then move to a different target. "This, and this, and then this." Pointing can be legato or staccato.
12. Point at a large object, for instance a painting. Then point at a detail in the painting. The gesture might be the same, but your intentionality and perception have changed.
13. Point at an object very near you; then point at something further away. Pointing can span a millimeter or hundreds of thousands of miles—for instance, if you point at the moon.

Figure 13.4 Focused pointing. Credit: Mojca-Peter.

14. Point at something while looking at something else. Fun or confusion?
15. Point for exclamatory joy: "Look, *there!*" Point for identification: "*That* one. No, the *other* one." Point for remonstration: "It was *you!*"
16. Make the pointing gesture, with the index finger extended. Now look at the extended finger, close or far, from various angles; and touch your pointing finger with your free hand. Isn't it amazing how much power there is to a pointing finger? And isn't it amazing to garner the finger's inherent power to play the piano, the cello, and any other instrument?

Let's be pretentious and say that pointing is an integrated embodiment of intentionality. Let's be even more pretentious and say that mastery of pointing is mastery of life itself (Figures 13.4 and 13.5).

Hot and cold

You've had thousands of experiences of hot and cold: showers and swimming pools, air conditioners and heaters, summers and winters, ovens and fans, ice-cold drinks and hot teas, chilling encounters with evil people and heartwarming encounters with delightful souls. A vast database of hot and cold lives in your body and your memory, but also in your imagination and your perception.

Figure 13.5 Distance pointing. Credit: Mojca-Peter.

1. Handle ice cubes. Hold an ice cube until it melts in your hand. Nest an ice cube between your hands. The ice cube will sting your hands with its coldness, but if you stick it out, your warm hands will melt the ice cube sooner or later.
2. Light a candle and put it down somewhere safe but within reach. Let your hand caress the vicinity of the flame. Depending on where you place your hand, you can capture a diffuse sense of heat with your open palm, or a focused point of burning heat directed at a precise point somewhere in your hand or finger.
3. Hold an ice cube with one hand and play with the heat from the candle with the other hand.
4. You can give someone a cold stare, analytical, distant, judgmental: icy to the core. And you can gaze at someone lovingly, with tenderness and warmth. Hot and cold sometimes start as physical or material properties, but they can also start as psychic energies.
5. The cold stare and the warm gaze may be spontaneous reflexes driven by an authentic emotion, perhaps combined with some intellectual control. But you know that you can generate heat and cold willingly. Playing an adagio by a Soviet composer whose music speaks of war and desolation, you imagine the Russian winter, destruction, despair, loneliness. And you play "cold." Other compositions, other musical phrases, other interpretations lead you to play "warm."

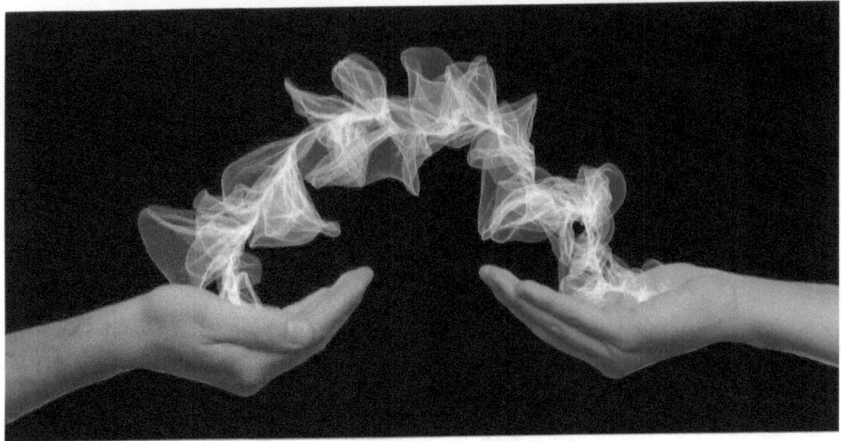

Figure 13.6 Hands of heat. Credit: Gerd Altmann.

6. You can literally blow hot and cold. Bring an open palm close to your mouth. Blow hot air at the palm, perhaps by whispering "aaaaahhhh." You know how to do it; the air will come out naturally warm from your insides and through your throat. Now blow cold air at your open palm. Again, you know how to do it; the air will come out cold because—well, because it will. Essentially, the difference lies in the air being stocked in your mouth (cold) or your throat (hot).
7. Imagine being naked outside during a snowstorm. Just a second or two of this imagined torture will make you shiver. Now imagine basking in the sun during a holiday at the beach. It doesn't matter if you don't enjoy beach holidays in real life; what matters is that your imagination has the power to make you hot or cold.
8. Sitting or standing, bring your hands together and intertwine your fingers; then bring the hands slightly apart and separate your fingers. Go back and forth between together and apart. Improvise reciprocal caresses with the hands. Squeeze the hands a little. Your hands will become ever cozier and comfier.
9. With cozy comfy clever hands, play the piano or the flute or any instrument in the world (Figures 13.6 and 13.7).

Light and heavy

Crumple a tissue paper into a ball, then park it in an open palm. You're holding nothing, supporting zero weight; the tissue paper is your teacher of lightness, of nothingness, of appreciating how little effort you need to hold

Figure 13.7 Hand of cold. Credit: Roland Mey.

something so light. Get a heavier object, like a paperweight or a piece of fruit. Place the piece of fruit on your open palm; now take the fruit away and put the tissue-paper ball in its place. You're practicing the art of light and heavy, of nothing and something.

Then apply what you've learned to handling your musical instrument. Place a crumpled tissue paper on a piano key, as a sort of reminder; now touch a piano key with as little weight as a tissue paper. You won't necessarily play the piano with this much weightlessness; you're only exercising gradation, from extremely light to extremely heavy and with a hundred intermediate shades in between (Figure 13.8).

A child who doesn't want to be picked can make herself amazingly heavy. By instinct and by trial and error, she lowers her center of gravity and makes her body floppy. Most importantly, she wills herself to become heavy. The same child also knows how to make herself fantastically light, demonstrating that there exist two types of weight: the material, measured by a scale in

Figure 13.8 Light. Credit: GRELOT71.

pounds and kilos; and the energetic, measured more subjectively but as real as the material weight.

There are small skinny people who take heavy thumping steps when they walk; there are morbidly obese people who dance with remarkable lightness. A guy wants a refund from a cashier; the cashier follows store procedure and refuses to refund the customer; the guy "won't budge," that is, he'll stay put and not even three other guys from security will make him leave.

Root yourself into the ground, and you'll become heavy. Mentally reach for the clouds, and you'll become light. Stay rooted downward and project your upper body upward, and you'll become both heavy and light at the same time (Figure 13.9).

Propagation and containment

A water fountain propagates energy outward, in paths determined by the design of the fountain and the water pressure. A magnet pulls energy inward toward itself, in paths determined by the size, strength, and placement of the magnet. These two material examples illustrate the opposition between propagating and containing, which we may also call putting it out and bringing it in, dispersing and gathering, releasing and holding (Figures 13.10 and 13.11).

Figure 13.9 Heavy. Credit: Felix Mittermeier.

Propagation is your voice reaching your listeners, your open hands making unconditional gifts, your generosity spreading outward; it's a way of saying "yes," a way of saying "it's allowed." At the extreme, it risks becoming loud, brash, invasive, chaotic, overwhelming. Containment is your capacity to gather your listeners' dispersed attention so that they really stay with the music; at the extreme, it's a way of saying "no," a way of saying "it's forbidden." Propagation invites uninhibited movement; at the extreme, it's disorganized and disorganizing. Containment invites economical movement; at the extreme, it's throttling and choking.

When you want to contain but you propagate instead, you're leaking energy. When you mean to propagate but you constrain instead, you're hoarding energy. Both are potentially explosive.

Figure 13.10 Propagation. Credit: ©Pedro de Alcantara.

Figure 13.11 Containment. Credit: Meredin.

Propagation and containment deserve their own book. Here we'll just practice a couple of simple exercises. Make a fist: it's containment. Relax the fist and open your palm: it's propagation. Shape and reshape your fist, passing from very tight to not so tight, from the tightest possible to the loosest possible. Where do you put your thumb? Under the fingers, above them, to their side. Make a medium-tight fist, then rotate your arm, lift and drop your arm, wave your arm; this shows you that a fist isn't a total-tightness project. Make a fist, then go punch something—a pillow, of course; and punch it sweetly, like a teasing friend. Make a fist, then use your other hand to caress, envelop, and squeeze the fist. Make two fists, and use them to practice your percussive skills, for instance at the piano or a tabletop, or by tapping one fist against the other. Make two fists, and shadowbox. Make two fists, then talk, sing, or produce sound effects while gesticulating with the fists.

The fist as a symbol of containment is much richer than we assume at first.

Open your palm. How many millimetric degrees of opening do you have at your disposal? How curved are your fingers, how concave, how convex? With two open palms, perform a silent dance by moving the hands here and there in front of you. With an open palm, rotate your arm slowly. Are you able to keep the open palm undisturbed, or does the rotation of the arm cause the shape of the open palm to change? Keep an open palm with one hand, and use the other to explore the open palm, caressing it, squeezing it, poking it. Keep an open palm and try to disturb its shape by squeezing it with the other hand. Can you resist the squeeze and keep the open palm constructed and fixed?

The open palm, our current symbol of propagation, is also richer than we might have assumed.

Pass quickly from a loose fist to a wide-open palm, then back to the fist again. Engage your two hands in a dancing dialogue. One will be Fist, the other will be Open Palm. Then they'll trade places. Variations, gradations, improvisations: Creative Health is the playful integration of propagation and containment. The goal isn't a middle point between two qualities, but a dynamic dialogue, a give-and-take that never stops.

Appearing and disappearing

In your life you've had to learn how to shrink and how to expand. You shrink to enter a car parked too close to another car, to ride public transportation during rush hour, to retrieve an object that has fallen behind an armoire. And you expand when you want to be seen by the waiter at a restaurant, when you need to protect a child from an incoming danger, when you want to tell a joke at a loud party. Some people are better at shrinking, others are better at expanding. But everyone is capable of at least some degree of shrinking and expanding. I think it's good to become alert to the phenomenon and to practice it, both in daily life and in your life as a musician.

We'll liken expanding and shrinking with appearing and disappearing. The peacock appears; the marmot disappears (Figures 13.12 and 13.13).

You can dress to appear big and dress to appear small—a loud outfit and a quiet outfit, as it were. You can sneak out of a party, and people will take a long time to realize you've disappeared. Waiting in line, you can impose yourself on someone who tries to cut in front of you. Listening to someone in distress, you can make your own problems disappear for a while, the better to witness and help the other.

Your field of perception shrinks and expands. You can tune out sounds and noises at a café; playing the cello in the back of an orchestra, you can zoom in on the clarinet, the bassoon, and the triangle. Your listening can travel, so to speak. And it can travel as if by itself, with a will of your own or thanks to your directed attention.

I attended a viola recital by a famous concert artist. Afterward, I went backstage to talk to the pianist, who was a friend of mine. I was surprised to see how small the violist was; on stage, she had given me the impression of being a big person. It's possible that she was in fact bigger on stage, with a stronger energy field, propagating self-assurance and the pleasure of performing for an

Figure 13.12 Appearing. Credit: Adil Abib.

Figure 13.13 Disappearing. Credit: Sergio Cerrato.

appreciative crowd. Or it's possible that I had made her physically bigger in my imagination because she played so authoritatively.

In my own performances, I aim to make my habitual self vanish before I go on stage. If possible, I take a nap the afternoon of the performance. The nap is a symbolic death. Then a new person is born, and it's this person that goes on stage and performs for me or in my place. A friend attended one of my house concerts. He told me that he saw me starting to disappear some minutes before the performance. I was socializing, talking to people, going here and there when my energy shifted; I became a sort of empty vessel that had enough room for that other person or entity to take my place. It's a paradox: I'm so little that I don't exist; I'm so spacious that I welcome a powerful presence inside me. The performance went very well.

I like making my cello disappear when I practice and play. I don't look at my hands or at the instrument itself; instead, I look into the void in front of me or left and right of me. With a little effort of the imagination, it's possible for me not to see the cello at all, not even with my peripheral vision. Then I become able to forget the cello's existence as an instrument. The cello dematerializes and becomes a space that's part of my space, rather than an object leaning against my body. The frontier between the cello and me disappears. And my doubts about playing the cello, my perceived difficulties regarding this or that passage of the repertoire, they too disappear with the cello. The Goddess of Nothing takes over; I become the loved child of the Goddess of Nothing, and I trust the Goddess of Nothing to play for me or through me. The feeling is difficult to describe, but it's a mixture of reassurance, joy, letting go, accepting and receiving, giving unconditionally, flowing, shining. To achieve it, I must stay out of the way of the Goddess of Nothing: no effort and no doubt, no huffing, no puffing, no extraneous gestures, no desire to impress the listeners, no fish to sell, nothing.

Energy, aesthetics, and psychology are intertwined. Some years ago, I met a musician who was having serious issues with one of his wrists. He was talented and accomplished, with a career spanning many decades. He told me that the player should dominate the instrument; playing was a battle of wills, and the player really had to show the instrument who was boss. To play was to dominate, and to dominate was a muscular affair. For him, the Goddess of Nothing would appear as a laughable absurdity. His playing was expressive and beautiful, I must say; and yet, it seemed clear to me that without a deep change in his aesthetics, his wrist was doomed, and probably his career, too (Figure 13.14).

Muscles in action are a sign of life. Effort helps you express and affirm your animality. Released by involved physical activity, endorphins and dopamine really do make you feel good! For some people, the absence of struggle is the

Figure 13.14 Fighting. Credit: Herbert Aust.

absence of excitement and meaning; struggle is life, and life is struggle. What to do if years of effort and struggle are now causing debilitating pain? For those who don't believe in the Goddess of Nothing, I suggest a compromise in two variations.

We'll imagine an archetypical or stereotypical martial artist who might be a practitioner of judo, aikido, taekwondo, or any other school, from the East or from the West. Our martial artist has a heightened physicality honed through decades of constant practice. Muscles are alive and well, the back is strong, the legs are strong, the arms are strong. But our martial artist's heightened physicality doesn't prevent or exclude a sense of directed energy, acknowledging the power of something that perhaps resides in the muscles but is born of attentiveness, of a relationship with space and breath. The compromise is to think of your beloved musical struggle as a martial arts bout in which the flow of energy and the sense of space are as present as the prized physicality. A little less muscle, a little more space—to the extent that you can.

The second version is for you to imagine your muscular, celebratory relationship with the instrument as a dance. We know how fit, how athletic, how well-built, and how flexible the best dancers really are. By conceptualizing your playing as a high-level dance, you can delight in your effort and yet allow for the flow of movement and energy (Figure 13.15).

Figure 13.15 Dancing . Credit: Pexels.

Latency

Inside your mind you hold many thousands of words you know, some of which you use frequently and others infrequently or never. The never-uttered words are held in reserve, at your disposal if one day you'd like to employ them. Words held in reserve are only one example of this phenomenon. You also hold thousands of gestures and motions inside your body, including a great many that you might never use. And you're capable of many emotions, even if in your daily life you express only a fraction of your total possibilities.

A large vocabulary of words makes it easier to communicate. A large vocabulary of gestures makes it easier to move. A large vocabulary of emotions makes it easier to live, even if you don't employ all the emotions at your disposal. I like using the word *latency* to refer to what you have in reserve, be they words, gestures, emotions, capabilities, money, books, objects, scores, and everything else in your life: for instance, latent words and latent gestures, ready to come out at a moment's notice. (In computing and other domains, *latency* means something else: the delay between a stimulus and a response.)

ENERGY

Energies are like words and gestures. Within you there exist many types of energies, some of which are constantly manifesting themselves in your life and your personality, others more intermittently. Much as you can stock up on words and gestures for future use, you can learn new energies and keep them in reserve. It doesn't mean that you become a bulging repository of too much energy, only that you become alert to the possibilities that lie within you. Latent energies are one of the best things for you to accumulate.

Catalog the qualities of energy that you're familiar with, and some unfamiliar ones for good measure. List the energies as opposing pairs. The simple act of making a list isn't banal. If you doubt me, list the Ten Commandments, in writing, in speech, or in song. List your siblings and cousins, by date of birth. List your favorite movies. List the cities and neighborhoods where you've lived. The list will light up all sorts of memory paths in your brain, a geography of emotions. You'll be in New York when you think of your years there, you'll be in São Paulo, in London, in Paris. It'll be quite a trip.

1. Heavy and light
2. Expanding and shrinking
3. Hot and cold
4. Wet and dry
5. Concentrated and diffuse
6. Friendly and hostile
7. Feminine and masculine
8. Grownup and childlike
9. Embracing and repelling
10. Loud and soft
11. Fast and slow
12. Rough and smooth
13. Static and dynamic
14. Rigid and flexible
15. Dense and sparse
16. Controlled and wild
17. Stable and unstable
18. Rounded and pointy
19. Active and passive
20. Stable and unstable
21. Bright and dim
22. Stagnant and flowing
23. Structured and improvised
24. Extroverted and introverted

Figure 13.16 Collected possibilities. Credit: Bernd Hildebrandt.

I don't claim to have all these energies latent inside me. But I do claim that playing with these concepts has deepened and broadened my practice of Creative Health (Figure 13.16).

Chapter 14

ANIMALITY AND HEALING

Meet your inner animal.

The inner animal isn't the same thing as your body. It's a sensorial and psychic being with agency, but with the tendency to sense first, think second; and, through sensation alone, arrive at a quick discernment: safe environment, I like it; unsafe environment, I'm outta here. Silk, linen, cotton, polyester: I don't know their names, but I can tell one from the other right away. And the thing called polyester, I don't like touching it, not with my fingers, not with my belly, not with my face.

The inner animal knows certain things before you know them yourself. And the inner animal knows certain types of things that you will never know; or, at least, not that part of you that thrives on analysis and understanding, that part of you that tends to issue a judgment before seeking an experience.

The inner animal breathes. While breathing, it senses the elastic movement of its breath, the elastic movement of its ribs and lungs, the elastic inflation and deflation occupying its trunk and affecting its whole being. There are plenty of human beings out there who are breathing normally, walking here and there, working, shopping, watching TV. And although they're breathing normally, they don't feel their elastic breaths going in and out of their elastic beings, and they don't feel their elastic ribs, and they don't think that their ribs deserve their attention. The inner animal is attentive and appreciative.

The inner animal wants to live, and it wants to live to the fullest; this is its urgency and its pleasure (Figure 14.1).

The inner animal has appetites, and the inner animal doesn't care to justify its appetites. Perhaps the inner animal doesn't comprehend the notions of justification, explanation, or apology. The appetite is what it is, not more, not less. The inner animal doesn't need to act upon its appetites every time that the appetite arises. The appetite is an energy that comes with sensations, pleasures, distractions; the animal might purr when the appetite arises. Purr or growl, we never know beforehand (Figure 14.2).

The inner animal receives information from sources other than books, the Internet, and all those fountains of useful and useless data. It's difficult to

Figure 14.1 Owl in flight. Credit: Danny Moore.

Figure 14.2 Purr and growl. Credit: Thomas Wolter.

describe rationally the workings of intuition, dreams, inklings, and nagging feelings that you can't pin down. But those workings are essential in everyone's lives and central to the life of the inner animal—much more central than the intellect or structured knowledge. The inner animal receives intuitive information and accepts its reception without questioning or doubting, and above all without ignoring or dismissing the information.

There's a big difference between the inner animal, whose intuition is reliable, and the adult who yearns for intuitive knowledge but lacks the essential conditions for receiving intuitive information. You can't trust your guts when your life is dominated by acquired habits, suppositions and judgments, dogmas and ideologies, and learned narrow-mindedness. The inner animal's gut feelings are probably very different from your own gut feelings.

The inner animal is innately playful. Farm animals, wild animals, animals in zoo enclosures, seagulls on beaches, pets, cats, dogs, animals both young and old: the urge to play is universal. Play is exploration, discovery, connection, conquest, courtship, and mating. Through play, the animal exerts and develops its intelligence. Also, play is play: in playfulness itself, there are uncountable pleasures, independent of developing one's intelligence or finding one's mate. Your inner animal doesn't think about playing, doesn't question whether playing is good or bad, doesn't regret playing, and doesn't suspend playing when the boss arrives at the office; play is so deeply rooted that it's no different from breathing and living. You probably know an adult human being who's shy about playing or downright hostile toward playfulness, be it verbal or physical. This adult friend of yours is in trouble and needs to reconnect to his or her inner animal (Figures 14.3 and 14.4).

The inner animal is a keen observer of the environment—not only the physical environment of places, spaces, sunlight, and rain, but the environment

Figure 14.3 Intuitive play. Credit: Anonymous via Pixabay.

Figure 14.4 Cat girl. Credit: Anonymous via Pixabay.

of other inner animals in interaction one with the other. The inner animal captures the soundscape of noises, music, speech, laughter, silence, machines, meowing, barking, the ever-changing symphony. You've seen a dog walking down the block and sensing, suddenly and reliably, that another dog is in the vicinity. You've seen a bird flying from window ledge to treetop to streetlamp, in a smooth continuity of perception and action. The adult in you has doubts and judgments that prevent your inner animal from moving in freedom.

The inner animal is drawn to animals and to the animalistic in objects, in works of art, in all aspects of daily life. The inner animal delights in a farmer's market, for instance; piles of fruits and vegetables, a festival of colors, shapes, tastes, and smells. The inner animal wants to take a bite of that luscious mango, partly because the mango is sweet and juicy, and partly because the inner animal wants to exercise its mandibles, its teeth, its tongue. The inner animal wants to peel a dozen carrots because they're carrots and the carrots are asking to be peeled, and the inner animal listens to the carrots and does the friendly thing toward those friendly vegetables. Your inner animal wants to touch, to squeeze, to caress; to kiss, to lick, to bite; to grab, to shake, to throw. Your inner animal is a dog, a cat, a bird, a little kid in eternal exploration and eternal interaction. There's a big difference between being bestial and being animal-like. Every animal has a bestial potential. Your beloved pussycat will one day go crazy over a bird or a mouse. But as regards your

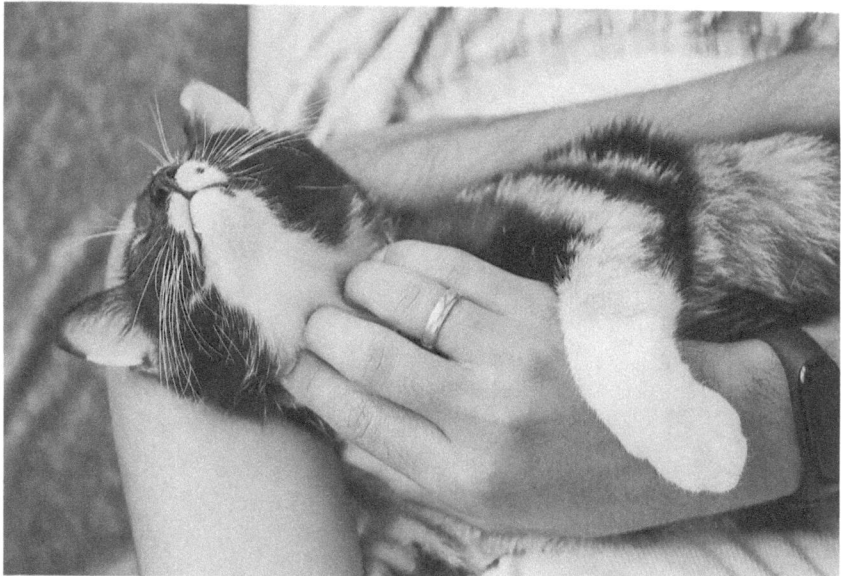

Figure 14.5 Cat being cuddled. Credit: Fuzzy Rescue.

inner animal, I'm not inviting you to maim and kill; I'm inviting you to sense and play (Figure 14.5).

Your inner animal has the hands, wrists, and fingers of the inner animal. They may look like the exact hands, wrists, and fingers that your adult self is familiar with. But this isn't the case. The stories that the inner animal tells about its hands are unlike your stories; the visual and tactile perceptions that the inner animal enjoys aren't the same, either. The inner animal has an informal mythology and theology regarding its hands, wrists, and fingers. These meaningful constructs are invisible and incomprehensible to your adult self. Imagine a baby discovering her hands for the first time: the marvel, the mystery, the strangeness, the beauty of my own hands; literally, I have no words to express what I feel; even if I did speak, I wouldn't be able to describe what I see and what I feel. The baby is the inner animal at work and play (Figures 14.6 and 14.7).

The Teddy Bear

Creative Health isn't literal-minded. It borrows the concept of animality from the zoological and biological domains and amplifies it, clothing it in symbolic, psychological, and mythological dimensions. You don't need a cat to be in the world of cats because you have Cat; you don't need a dog because you

Figure 14.6 Paw and hand. Credit: giselastillhard.

Figure 14.7 Animal and child. Credit: Lenka Novotná.

have Dog; you have Horse, Parrot, Snake, Lion; you have many potentialities that you can connect with by indirect means. Among the available means, I advocate the stuffed animal as a tool of healing for all people, including all adults.

We're used to seeing young children playing with teddy bears and other stuffed animals, and we think that the children and their teddy bears are terribly cute together. But there's something else at work that goes beyond the cute. A young child's connection with animality, with her own inner animal, goes deep. The young child is animistic by birth. She sees every object as having a soul and a personality, a story to tell; and the object is talking to her, perhaps in English, perhaps in a nonverbal language. The young child perceives magic in the quotidian: it's incredible that water flows from taps, it's wonderful that a pencil can make drawings; it's amazing that the teddy bear understands her so well and loves her unconditionally. In her interactions with stuffed toys, the child works through her emotions, her hopes and fears, her need for companionship, for being witnessed, seen, and heard.

The relationship between the child and the stuffed toy is sensorial and immediate. The teddy bear offers the child a wealth of textures, from its hairy coat to its core, which is both firm and elastic. The teddy bear is huggable, squeezable, and snuggable. The huggable and hugged teddy bear enhances the sensations that the child has about her own self, her body, her hands, wrists, and fingers (Figure 14.8).

Figure 14.8 Child and teddy. Credit: Petra.

Do you want to feel good? Squeeze a teddy bear. Do you want comfort and companionship? Squeeze a teddy bear. Do you want to overcome the fear of ridicule? Squeeze a teddy bear. Do you want your hands, wrists, and fingers to receive a healing session from an experienced and caring professional? Squeeze a teddy bear. Squeeze it and caress it, pull on its ears, throw it and catch it, let it lie on your chest as you take a nap.

The teddy bear is just an example. Cat, dog, lion, elephant, sheep, goat, it doesn't matter. An old cashmere sweater can be your teddy bear, too. If you're literal-minded, your hands, wrists, and fingers work in a certain way; if you're imaginative, your hands, wrists, and fingers work in a different way.

Enveloping

Our days are punctuated by the gesture of enveloping. If you send a check by mail to someone, you'll literally envelop the check. Wrap a gift, and you'll envelop the gift. Tuck a young child in bed, and you'll envelop the child with a blanket and with your caring attention. We adults can hardly imagine how good the child feels when we envelop her. We like being enveloped ourselves, but the child's thoughts and feelings probably go deeper than ours. Protection, comfort, reassurance, safety; the sensorial pleasure of the blanket and its textures; the feeling of being acknowledged by the adult; the invitation to relax, to sleep, to rest, to let go. Place some papers in a folder; this, too, is enveloping. Intertwine two clean socks, tucking them together. Put clothes on, and you envelop yourself. Wintry night, and you go out wearing thermal underwear, a flannel shirt, a cashmere sweater, a woolly hat, leather gloves, a coat, socks, and boots: you're enveloped from head to toe, you're comfortable and safe, you look good and you feel good. When you put an instrument in its case, you envelop it and make it safe from the elements, from accidents, from danger (Figure 14.9).

Become attentive to the phenomenon of envelopment, at home, in private, in public. Keep an informal catalog of what you see and what you do with envelopment: mango wrapped in paper, baby wrapped in cloth, hand wrapped in glove, foot wrapped in sock; gifts wrapped in paper, purchases wrapped in bubble wrap; your brain enveloped by your skull, your mind enveloped by concentration and focus.

Wrap your arms across your chest, enveloping your chest and its precious contents: the heart, the lungs, the ribs; your breath, your emotions, your vulnerabilities, your stories. Wrap your arms across the chest, and you express something about your masculinity and your femininity; wrap your arms, and your posture might express any and every emotion: confidence, rebellion,

Figure 14.9 Enveloped baby. Credit: Adele Morris.

displeasure, coquetry. Wrap your arms and dance; wrap your arms and sing; wrap your arms and think (Figures 14.10 and 14.11).

Make a loose fist with your right hand and wrap your left hand around it. This is the *shaolin salute*. Make and release your fist, looking at your hand like a child sensing her fist for the first time. Practice gradations of looseness and tightness. Make the fist, release it; repeat. With a loose fist, rotate your

Figure 14.10 Enveloped flowers. Credit: Thinh Nguyen Gia.

Figure 14.11 Enveloped chest. Credit: Aathif Aarifeen.

arm and lift your hand, as a sort of dance. Thanks to your imagination and initiative, have your hand give birth to a sentient being called Fist. Then put a fermata on the fist: hold it in relaxed wonderment. Now bring the other hand around it, touching it tenderly, not wrapping it just yet: the approach of hand to fist is like a dance of courtship, one trying to mesmerize the other.

Touch and caress, wrap gently for a second, let go; touch and caress, wrap, let go; the wrapping, which is a kind of hold, contains its own release; the hold isn't a choke. And at some point, wrap and hold: settle the wrapping dance into a sweet fermata. Let it happen when the hands are ready for it, when their dance allows it and invites it. You aren't doing the one and only shaolin salute; you're improvising variations on the theme of the shaolin salute. The official salute, so to speak, is specific; your improvisations are general. The official salute requires that you make the fist with the right hand. Your improvisations might ignore the requirement. Make a left fist and start the dance all over again.

Wrap your arms around your chest and place your hands under your armpits. How firmly, how softly; for how long, for how short? Are your hands going to squeeze your pectorals or are they going to leave them alone? Are your armpits going to squeeze the hands tight, or are they going to envelop the hands with gentle warmth? The hands, enveloped by the friendly armpits, are like a baby enveloped in a blanket: safe and comfortable. I know it sounds like a joke, but wrapping your hands under your armpits might help heal the tired hands, the overworked hands, the hurt hands (Figure 14.12).

A Leap of the Imagination

The imagination is the most powerful force in our lives. We imagine problems and solutions, we imagine systems of thought and belief, we imagine futures, we imagine people and dialogues, we imagine what it must have been like for Mozart to improvise a cadenza while performing a piano concerto. The list of things we constantly imagine is infinite.

If you imagine that you have a rash on the skin on the back of your hand, it's possible that the rash will take on some sort of existence in your eyes and feelings, although the dermatologist assures you that there is nothing, absolutely nothing wrong with your skin.

If you imagine that your hand is too small to play certain stretches on the instrument, it's possible that your hand will become a bit smaller and tighter, obeying your imagination. Then the hand confirms that it is small and tight, and it confirms that you can't do this or that action.

Figure 14.12 Enveloping love. Credit: Ian Lindsay.

With a little imagination, your hands can become "like a cat," supple and flexible, capable of fast sudden actions. Your hands can become "like a bird," "like a rabbit," "like a horse." The animal is intuitive, adaptable, strong. It acts on impulse, without analytical calculations or judgments. Circulation and breathing, locomotion, all the biological functions work as manifestations of nature. The animal has rhythm pulsing in its veins, the flow of life pushing and pulling inside its being. It's wonderful when your hands become "like a cat," or like any animal suited to your purposes (Figure 14.13).

Let's take our imaginations farther. It's useful to think of your hands not as "like animals," but as animals themselves. If you keep animals in the house,

Figure 14.13 Animal hand. Credit: Torgeir.

you know that they have their own thoughts and feelings, their habits and histories, their behaviors and energies. The animals acknowledge your presence and return your love, but they don't exist exclusively in relation to your love; they have their own agendas. I think you'd benefit from thinking of your hands in this way.

One of the amazing capabilities of animals is their potential for self-healing. Let's suppose a deer is shot by a hunter. The bullet rips through one of the deer's shoulders but doesn't kill it. The deer escapes into the forest and hides from the world. It rests, it breathes, it processes its sensations over days and weeks. Perhaps the deer fasts, perhaps it sleeps for a long time. The details don't matter; the important thing is that the deer survives and heals all by itself with the help of Mother Nature.

The animal, then, has a potential for self-healing. It also has the capacity to offer healing to other animals, to its young for instance, but even to animals of other species. We know of stories in which a chimp adopts an orphan kitten, or an abused dog who's befriended by a parrot and overcomes the trauma of cruelty and abandonment thanks to its playful new friend.

Figure 14.14 Splashing animal. Credit: Roman Kogomachenko.

Figure 14.15 Lighted hand. Credit: Michael Treu.

If you think of your hands as animals, you might see and sense—you might believe—that your hands have self-healing potential, as well as the potential to offer healing to other parts of your body and to your friends, spouses, lovers, children, patients, and so on. We go to the doctor for a checkup, and the doctor palpates our abdomen and takes our pulse, and if the doctor is any good, we start feeling better simply because of her expert, confident, health-giving touch. You don't need to be a trained professional for your hands to offer healing to yourself and to others.

And with those hands that are loving and lively animals, full of warmth and healing, you play the violin or the cello or any other instrument (Figures 14.14 and 14.15).

Chapter 15

RITUAL

Daily life is a succession of informal rituals. Go visit your own imaginary day, and I'll be your witness. The bed in which you sleep, alone or in company, is a ritualistic territory that encompasses two worlds and many countries: the world of day and the world of night, the countries of rest, renewal, dreams, agitation, intimacy, insomnia, past, present, and future. You wake up, or you find yourself awake; this in itself is a rite of passage, banal, ordinary, but a rite of passage nevertheless: you pass from night to day, from receptive subconsciousness to acquisitive consciousness, from no goals to goals.

Homework: Ritualize your bedroom, your bed, and your sleep.

Coffee or tea, it doesn't matter; preparing the drink is ritualistic, the cup is talismanic. Every object exists in the material domain and in the symbolic domain. Your mug might be a cheap one from the dollar store, but it's the child of Cup: the archetype of vessels and containers, of bowls and steins, of goblets and chalices. Perhaps you don't see your mug as the child of Cup. But it'd break your heart if you accidentally broke it; and it'd really, really upset you if someone else broke it. And when you hold the cup that holds the liquid, you receive—from the cup and the liquid, and from your hands and fingers—a sort of kaleidoscopic, magnetized memory of every cup you've ever touched and every coffee or tea you've ever drunk.

Your hand, holding an ordinary mug or a special one, is Hand, holding Cup. And Hand holding Cup is a potent ritual, depicted in mosaics from Pompeii, still lifes from the Dutch Golden Age, countless scenes in novels, films, and plays, thousands of ads for thousands of products. Hand holding Cup is an eternal story, and every day you live the eternal story anew. The musician in you benefits from being alert to the cup, its shape and weight; to the difference between a full cup and an empty cup, the difference between a cup holding a hot liquid and a cup holding something lukewarm. "My coffee is cold." This might be the start of a poem, a country song, a Lied.

Did you know that Johann Sebastian Bach wrote a secular cantata about coffee? "Schweigt stille, plaudert nicht," BWV 211, composed in around 1734. Its title translates as "Keep quiet, don't chatter."

Homework: Ritualize your breakfast, with special emphasis on the hot drink and its cup (Figure 15.1).

Bathing, showering, drying your hair, brushing your teeth: these are daily informal manifestations of Ablution. We want never to forget the connection between the banal shower and the not-so-banal baptism, the not-so-banal cleansing before entering a temple, the not-so-banal preparations before one's wedding. Different cultures and religions assign different degrees of importance to cleanliness, but probably there are no cultures or religions in which cleanliness doesn't play at least some role. The daily gesture is representative of something bigger than itself.

I don't mean that you should spend half an hour brushing your teeth. The paradox of ritualistic integration is that the ordinary can become extraordinary without changes in context, rhythm, or duration. Taking time to do things is often good and necessary, but the real change comes not from the clock but from the heart. You perceive the gesture as elevated; you enjoy it; you smile to yourself when you do it because you don't completely forget Pompeii and J. S. Bach and the incredible intertwined web of events, stories, and memories that are culminating right now, with your drinking tea or brushing your teeth.

Homework: Ritualize your personal hygiene and grooming (Figure 15.2).

Waking up, showering and shaving, making coffee, having breakfast. The day continues, and every step along the way you'll be doing something banal

Figure 15.1 Coffee cup. Credit: Anja.

Figure 15.2 In the river. Credit: Sasin Tipchai.

and not so banal. Attitude elevates your day. Your hands, wrists, and fingers are engaged throughout the day in allowing the ritual to unfold. The hands are the godparents of the ritual. Let's go further and say that the hands themselves are the ritual.

Here's an exercise. Decide that you will, in fact, lengthen your toothbrushing session for the sake of study. Give your life an imaginary soundtrack, choosing its lyrics carefully. Below is an imaginary translation of an imaginary stanza of an imaginary secular cantata by the not-so-imaginary Johann Sebastian Bach. The cantata is titled "Deine Zähne, ach, solch engelhafte Perlen." (You don't need to look it up on the Internet; this cantata doesn't exist.)

> Memory and story,
> art and history,
> mystery, pleasure, joy,
> wonderment, gratitude:
> brush your teeth.

Handle the brush, the toothpaste, the tap; open and close the tube of toothpaste, sense the volume of the tube and its form, its texture. Squeeze the tube so very gently that no toothpaste squirts out. Then squeeze it a little harder, until a bit of toothpaste becomes visible, like a groundhog checking out the weather and deciding to come out of its hole or not. The tube is designed and manufactured by a team of professionals. It's made attractive to the eye. Would you want to brush your teeth using a black tube with a drawing of a squished cockroach on it? Look at the tube, read everything that is printed on it. If you want to be a good little student, memorize everything on it and then recite it or sing it in the style of "Deine Zähne" by the incomparable J. S. Bach. To the alert touch, the tube of toothpaste is a marvel. It invites caress, it welcomes attention, it responds to your thoughts as your thoughts become gestures. Your handling of the tube is a revealing self-portrait. This is a fact. Your housemate squeezes the tube all wrong, leaving it shapeless and untidy. And you can't stand seeing the tube all deformed, and you're seriously considering moving out. Or getting a divorce.

The brush is the child of Brush. You wouldn't want to brush your teeth with a bristly broom, but it's useful to notice how the two objects are related in design, construction, and form. The healthy hand is an expert in bristles, in their resistance and elasticity, in their liveliness. Dead or dying bristles are no fun. A toothbrush can give you the creeps. Inertia, negligence, and laziness have stopped you from replacing the horrible toothbrush, but the day comes when you can't take it any longer.

> Hands, wrists, fingers;
> bristles, gums, teeth;
> toothpaste, water.
> The dancers are ready.

The musician in you imagines a mélodie by Claude Debussy with lyrics by Paul Verlaine, a Taylor Swift song, a pastiche, a jingle, a chant. The main thing is for your mind and heart to be alert to the moment and to its infinite possibilities. The hands, wrists, and fingers behave differently when the mind is attentive and the heart is warm. I know that most days you must get out of the house and rush to work. It really isn't necessary to take this much time to brush your teeth. You're stretching the clock as homework, as a meditation, as a joke that isn't really a joke. You're having a ritualistic experience in a territory where normally you don't pay attention to the moment. But the moment is full of possibilities (Figure 15.3).

Sink design, tap design: your home has a few sinks and a few taps, and it's worth your while noticing how the taps look and how they behave. Place yourself next to the sink. Now close your eyes and caress the tap, up and down, up and down. Sense its shape and size; sense its material. Artists have taken this specific material and made beautiful things with it—remarkable things, impressive things. In some ways, every tap is beautiful because it's the child of Tap. Your hands explore the child of Tap, your inner J. S. Bach

Figure 15.3 Child drawing. Credit: Thomas G.

composes a cantata, and you feel many things for the first time or as if for the first time. Up to now, you've taken your taps for granted; you've used them, opened and closed them, and sometimes you were irritated with a leaking tap. But have you really sensed your taps and communed with their form and function? If not, you've denied your hands, wrists, and fingers the pleasure of handling a special object with a shape and size like no other in the house.

> Brush: hold.
> Toothpaste tube: squeeze.
> Tap: open.
> Minty goodness, thank you,
> Danke schön, merci.

Homework: Ritualize the fixtures in your home.

The ritualistic experience is full of contradictions and paradoxes. A thing can be itself and its own parody. I'm making up some jokey poems about brushing teeth. Maybe the poems are so jokey as to be downright stupid—a parody of bad poetry. At the same time, my alertness to these ordinary objects and actions keeps increasing. I do see the tube of toothpaste as something interesting; I do enjoy my time opening and closing the tap; I do feel moved brushing my teeth. And my hands, wrists, and fingers keep getting more skillful, more delicate, more creative all day long, day after day.

Your music life includes hundreds of actions that deserve the ritualistic treatment. Opening the cover of a piano keyboard takes half a second and requires no thought, no effort—except that you could potentially drop the cover on your fingers or the fingers of a child; it has happened more than once in the history of music. Taking a cello out of its case is a sort of dance, sometimes awkward, sometimes smooth. The design of the cello case can help or hinder. The case might feel unbalanced and wobbly when upright, so you put it down every time you take the cello out or put it back in. The cello case is talking to you, and you're talking back to it. Ritual is a dialogue.

I think you ought to punctuate your days, weeks, and months with the clock-stretching meditation where you do something more slowly and carefully than usual; where you open your cello case not because you need to take the cello out but because you want to practice the art of opening the cello case: open and close, open and close again, like a child who finds a mechanism fascinating and explores the mechanism in itself, by itself, for itself.

Your attentive hands, having learned from the ritualistic experience and having elevated the banal gesture to a not-so-banal Gesture, your attentive hands opening and closing the cello case are the same hands that will touch the cello and the bow, producing exquisite vibrations (Figure 15.4).

Homework: Ritualize opening and closing your instrument case.

Open the violin case: ritual. Take the bow in your hands: ritual. The "bowness of the bow" enhances your attention and pleasure. This bow is the apex of

Figure 15.4 Cellist. Credit: Ri Butov.

centuries of human experimentation, going back to the first bow that someone, somewhere imagined and created. (Historians say that the first musical bow appeared in Mongolia.) And now the bow is in your hands, the magical and mystical bow, which we'll name Bow. Materials: pernambuco wood, carbon fiber, horsehair, mother-of-pearl, ivory, steel, plastic; how can you ever forget that to play the cello is to handle horsehair and mother-of-pearl? Tighten the bow hair: ritual. Rosin to horsehair: ritual. Rosin is a form of resin, a sticky substance that comes from trees and is similar to sap but different from it. Sap is used to make syrup and medicines; resin is used to make varnish and glazes. Rosin is made by heating fresh liquid resin until it becomes solid. It smells a bit like pine and has a glassy, orange look, sometimes light, sometimes dark. Technically, a chunk of rosin is called a "cake of rosin."

Like horsehair, pernambuco, and mother-of-pearl, rosin connects you to nature. It manifests the transformation of nature by human creativity, by the artistic and spiritual impulse. Handling rosin, smelling it, looking at it, and marveling at how pretty the cake of rosin really is; the helpful, loving rosin allows you to play the cello, express yourself, and connect to the timeless Creative Source. Rosin invites its rituals; rosin deserves its rituals. Rosin should be called "Wonderment and Gratitude." And the principle applies across the board: to handling clarinet and oboe reeds, handling the varnished guitar, and handling the maple, pearwood, or ebony recorder.

Homework: Ritualize the preparation of your daily practice (Figure 15.5).

Figure 15.5 Brushing a horse. Credit: Alexa.

Folding and unfolding a music stand is an ancient and archaic ritual. Opening a score: ritual. Turning a page: ritual. Writing down a fingering or a breath mark: ritual. Tuning an instrument: ritual. Hands, wrists, and fingers, working together to turn a guitar peg in small increments, comma by comma until you hear the just intonation of the perfect interval: ritual.

More than forty years ago, I witnessed an event that I'll never forget. I attended a concert by Egberto Gismonti, the Brazilian pianist, guitarist, improviser, and composer. The first piece in the program was an acoustic guitar duo, with both guitars amplified. I apologize for not remembering the name of the second guitarist, sitting to the left of Gismonti. Looking at each other and smiling, the two of them tuned their guitars. They started the piece; Gismonti heard some little problem with his amplifier; while strumming the guitar's open strings with his right hand, he reached out with his left hand and tweaked the amplifier; all the while, he kept looking at his friendly colleague, smiling, smiling, smiling. And then the two of them resumed their performance, although in truth they never interrupted it. The amplifier tweak happened in a completely ritualistic manner, respecting the stage, the public, and music itself.

Homework: Ritualize the occupation of the stage when performing.

In ritual, we don't take things for granted. "It's just a glass of wine." No, it's a lot more than just a glass of wine. "It's just your fingers touching the piano." No, it's a lot more. Ritual is the whole person, invested in the moment and in its symbolic charge. Investment can be lighthearted, light-bodied, graceful; investment doesn't mean an intensity of effort. But investment is always quite different from the lack of investment.

Ritual is an awareness of the threads connecting the thing being ritualized with the whole of your life, and an awareness of the threads connecting the whole of your life with the whole of Life. The awareness and appreciation are like the skin on your body: it exists; you feel it; you move with it, breathe with it, commune with it (Figure 15.6).

A child is playing with a toy. Her ritual is innocent yet elevated. We find it terribly touching, and we want to venerate the child and love her unconditionally; we want to express our emotions, having witnessed something that we consider cute and adorable but that we should consider integrated, coherent, pure, and perfect. Child, object, context, moment; beauty and meaning; the paradox of this unique child in this precise moment, doing a precise gesture with a precise object, and yet triggering in us indescribable perceptions of timelessness and universality.

Homework: Learn from the wisdom of children.

From drinking a cup of coffee to performing on stage, your hands, wrists, and fingers are vital instruments of ritual. But let's not forget the rituals in

RITUAL 229

Figure 15.6 Blowing bubbles. Credit: Daniela Dimitrova.

Figure 15.7 Ritualized life. Credit: Ri Butov.

which the hands themselves become the center of ritual. Trying on fancy gloves for size at the upmarket boutique; trying on cheap woolly gloves from the market stall: these are two versions of the same ritual. Trimming and filing your nails, applying polish, removing a hangnail. Washing your hands before eating, while cooking, after going to the toilet: let's call this "before, while, after," abbreviating the huge number of times you wash your hands and the huge number of reasons to do it. Coming home from a very cold day and running your hands under warm water. Smashing your finger and running it under cold water, the better to start the healing process. Agitatedly washing your hands because you touched something mushy and mysterious. Spraying your hands with hydrogel because germs are flying around and attempting to contaminate everyone in sight.

A funeral is an important ritual. Trimming your nails is an insignificant ritual—unless you understand that *every* ritual is a manifestation of Ritual, the melding of awareness, commitment, connection, elevation, and grace.

Homework: Ritualize Life (Figure 15.7).

Chapter 16

KNOWLEDGE AND MYSTERY

There's a moment every dawn when the night starts dissipating and the day affirms itself, tentatively at first. The light falling upon the city is special, hazy, otherworldly. You're walking to the bakery down the block from your home, along the usual sidewalk, with the usual traffic going by next to you. But the light is so strange that you might feel that you're in a movie set, where a story is being enacted and you are part of it, and you don't really know your lines or what the director expects from you. The experience is a bit dreamlike, a bit hallucinatory. "It's night and it's day, at the same time; it's both, or maybe neither. I don't know exactly where I am, and I don't know exactly who I am" (Figure 16.1).

We'll call this a *liminal experience*. The word "liminal" means "of or pertaining to a threshold." It's related to the word "limit," which some scholars say might be related to the Latin word "limus," which means "transverse, oblique." I'll put the dictionary aside and I'll compose a little poem instead:

Liminal: threshold,
frontier, portal,
brink, window;

porous, confusing,
ambiguous, oblique,
scary, exciting.

The liminal territory, which isn't necessarily an actual place in space, joins two seemingly separate or opposite states. The liminal experience consists in being in between two states or spaces, belonging to both at the same time (Figure 16.2).

Stand by an open window, with one ear facing out onto the street and the other facing in toward the room. Now you're ambiguously inside and outside, between the two spaces and belonging to both. You may well feel ambivalent about it, perhaps confused or threatened by something difficult to describe. It's also possible that you'll feel transported and energized because certain

Figure 16.1 Liminality. Credit: Luca Finardi.

limits between you and the world have been lessened or even erased. You might feel "bigger," or "freer," "more powerful," "lighter," "more open."

You perform a cadenza to a Classical concerto, improvised and yet organic, in the style and language of two hundred and fifty years ago and yet completely of the moment. I count it as a liminal experience, bridging the gap between the left and right brains, between now and then, between you and not-you. We might reasonably count all creative spurs as liminal experiences, belonging to this material and immediate world and also to that other world, immanent, inexplicable.

Elvis Presley was both his authentic self and the knowing parody of himself, both god and clown, both profane and religious, both very White and very not White, both a serious musician and a performer who didn't take himself seriously. His identity as a performer was fluid; Elvis was a herald of the liminal, and he took his adoring audience into the liminal territory with him. Elvis is just an example. The performance space is a liminal territory by definition.

Passing from backstage to the stage is a liminal experience. Standing at the threshold of the stage, invisible to the public but visible to the stagehands, you're seen and not seen at the same time. At that moment, your perception of yourself might also be divided. The experience is creepy and marvelous; you like it, and you don't like it; you might, you just might fail utterly once you

Figure 16.2 A liminal entity. Credit: fr.m.wikipedia.org.

enter the stage; you might, you just might play in a special way, very different from the practice room or the rehearsal (Figure 16.3).

Passing from backstage to the stage is a specialized version of a wider phenomenon: passing from the private sphere to the public one. By yourself at home, you're in a private space having private thoughts. If you leave your home, you enter a public space. It doesn't matter if the street is quiet and no

Figure 16.3 A liminal passage. Credit: Ariel Hii.

one is watching you or reaching out to you; the space has changed, and you're likely to think and feel a little differently, too. There are some very private individuals who find every public space uncomfortable, but there are also individuals who are comfortable in the public sphere and discombobulated in private. The main thing is that the private and public spheres are distinct, and the passage from one to the other and back again isn't banal. Between the two spheres, there's a threshold, sometimes as clear and plain as a door, sometimes less clear or less plain. I'd say that every threshold is liminal, and I'd include all doors, windows, corridors, and stairways in my list of liminal territories inviting the liminal experience.

Passing from playing metronomically to playing in tempo rubato is a liminal experience, sometimes queasy, sometimes liberating. Being ready to do something and not being ready is a typical liminal experience. Taking an exam or playing an audition is an enhanced liminal experience. There are situations where you feel certain that you're doing something on your own initiative while feeling just as certain that some difficult-to-name power is compelling you to do that very thing. This is a deeply meaningful liminal experience, where you're straddling the ego and the absence of ego.

Let's say you put on a concert dress or suit, feeling that it's a silly obligation borne out of convention, feeling that it's uncomfortable and it doesn't make sense and you don't look good in the dress or suit; then finding your attitude and discourse changing, partly as the result of your wearing a "monkey suit." You don't believe in the effects that your manner of dress can have on your perception of yourself and the world; and yet you can't deny that the manner of dress has obvious and remarkable effects. If both are true at the same time, putting on a concert dress and taking it off become liminal experiences.

My late father was a doctor trained in a certain tradition of numbers, measurements, and statistics; of the notion of the human body as a machine and as a conduit for chemistry; of localized symptoms requiring localized attention; of a never-questioned separation between the physical and the psychological; of the clinical truth, proved and not to be disproved.

At some point he had a herniated disk and suffered a lot of pain. He tried the usual remedies—that is, the usual painkillers, enforced rest, and physical therapy of his tradition—but the pain persisted. One of his former students had trained as an acupuncturist after finishing medical school, and he offered to treat my father with daily sessions. Reluctantly, my father decided to give it a go. To his surprise and puzzlement, the sessions lessened his pain. His paradigm, his clinical truth measured and forever proved, didn't acknowledge the existence of acupuncture meridians, of yin and yang, of heaven and earth. Meridians didn't make any sense! And yet here he was, confronted with a challenge to his belief system and to his certainties. It was a liminal experience.

I think it's useful to sense the phenomenon in its multiple manifestations, to sense your response to the phenomenon, to accept and to embrace the liminal experience—first because the experience is inevitable, and second because embracing it enhances your life in many ways. Becoming comfortable, or relatively comfortable, with ambiguity is a sort of victory; resisting and resenting ambiguity is a defeat and a loss.

Alertness to liminality increases the enjoyment of life. Ambiguity triggers creative reactions. The confused left brain, to some extent invaded by the right brain, has a symbolic nervous breakdown—with the best possible results. It works the other way, too: the right brain feels intimidated by incomprehensible demands from a lunatic drill sergeant, foaming at the mouth with needless questions and commands. And the mushy right brain is shaken into some sort of order.

We all pass through unbelieving to believing, and the other way around: from believing to unbelieving. The passage between one and the other is a liminal experience, unfolding in a foggy landscape. I believed that a certain famous cellist was a marvelous musician; then I changed my mind, and I don't believe it anymore. I believed that musicians had to be faithful to the scores that they interpreted, and then I started feeling that the philosophy was ill-defined and difficult to put into practice. Then I started feeling that faithfulness to the score was a sort of trap for the mind, and no one knew what it meant or how to do it. Playing Bach on the modern piano: yes, or no? I say yes. Rewriting Bach? I say yes. Everybody is rewriting Bach every time they play any of his compositions. It's a kind of psychosis not to understand that to perform is to rewrite.

In your life, examples abound of the change of mind, which is a change of belief. And the change of mind necessarily implies a change in behavior. The hands, wrists, and fingers of the musician who's faithful to the score are different from the hands, wrists, and fingers of the unfaithful and the faithless. This isn't to say that the hands of the unfaithful are superior or inferior to those of the faithful, only that they are different. You can confirm this for yourself, by playing varied interpretations of the same piece. Try to play well, and you behave in a certain way. Try to impress a teacher, and you play in another way. Try to mock the composer or the audience, and you play in yet another way.

There's a way of dealing with ambiguity and ambivalence, in and around the liminal territory. And it's also a way of dealing with the demonstrably absurd. It's to believe it and not believe it at the same time; to not believe it and yet agree to play a game with it. Let's call it "dancing with the absurd" (Figure 16.4).

Figure 16.4 Stepping into the void. Credit: Melissa G.

We'll take palm reading as an example. For the sake of argument, we won't discuss whether it's a totally absurd pursuit or if it's based on demonstrable and reliable principles. But let's say that you do think of palm reading as an absurd waste of time and a danger because people in distress consult wicked palm readers and let themselves be bamboozled. And let's say you meet a friendly stranger at a party who takes hold of your hand without asking you for permission and starts analyzing your palm and telling you things about yourself, your past, your present, and your future. The liminal experience that I propose is for you to go along with it as a lark at a party. (Remember, this is all happening in your imagination.) You don't believe in it and you reject it; and here you are, playing with it or playing at it.

The willingness to play with the stranger triggers the thoughts and feelings that willingness alone can trigger. These thoughts and feelings are different from those of unwillingness. The novel encounter brings novel perceptions: for instance, of someone holding your hand and looking at it closely, running a finger along the lines of your palm while saying incomprehensible or meaningless things to you and about you (Figure 16.5).

The friendly stranger is a foil to your unbelief and a mirror to your behaviors, a guide taking you somewhere you don't want to go. But to a certain extent, you go there, "as a lark." I'm not asking you to believe in palmistry, only to explore the liminal experience and confront yourself with the absurd

Figure 16.5 Lined palm. Credit: wal_172619.

or seemingly absurd, the equivocal or seemingly equivocal, the ambiguous, the unknown.

Had you rejected the liminal experience and told the friendly stranger to let go of your palm, you'd have missed out on some interesting possibilities—not in palmistry itself, but in the encounter with the liminal and the responses inside you that the liminal allows and encourages.

Your hands, wrists, and fingers are heralds of the liminal. They are so rich in talent, skill, knowledge, and memory that we can't begin to comprehend what they can do—what they can ultimately, completely, utterly do. Psychomotor

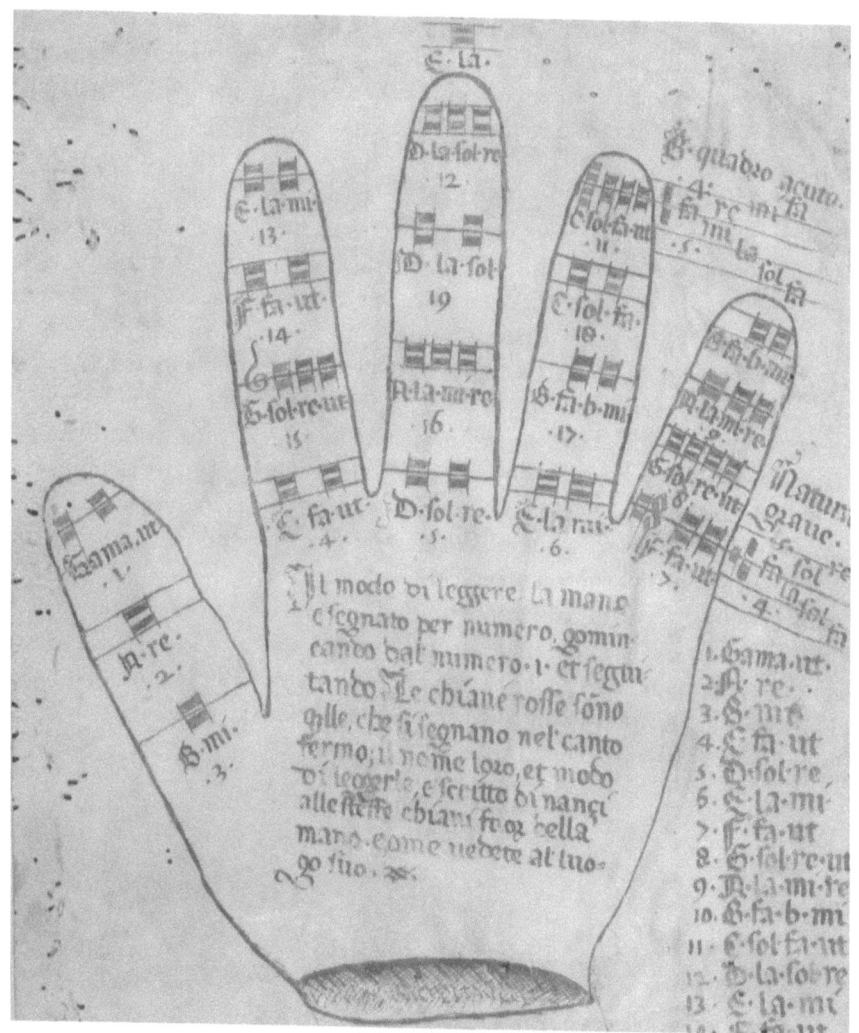

Figure 16.6 The Guidonian hand. Credit: en.wikipedia.org.

skills and instrumental techniques that you've developed through decades of practice are only one dimension of your hands. Their capacity to sense and to react; their capacity to give and receive pleasure; their capacity to express everything, from the worst insults to the most elevated discourse; their sheer magnificent importance in your life; all of it intertwined in a totality of possibilities. Approaching and accepting liminality, you'll be better able to assess or perceive the totality in which your hands express themselves. Totality is the power that heals a hurt hand, and liminality is one tool among many to help you accept and embody the totality (Figure 16.6).

Liminality is a territory of paradoxes involving the hands, wrists, and fingers. "I'm aware of how I gesticulate when I talk, I'm not aware; both are true." "I'm deciding how to use my hands, my hands are themselves deciding what they want to do; both are true." "I like my hands, I don't like my hands; both are true." From time to time you catch a glimpse of your hand doing something, and you see it as if for the first time: a strange hand, the hand of a stranger. "It's my hand, it's not my hand, both are true."

A simplification reduces a complex idea to something easier to grasp, but it risks distorting the idea, misinterpreting it, misusing it. Exaggerating the risk, we'll say that every simplification is a lie. But simplification is a useful tool in many settings, particularly when you announce to your own self (out loud or just in your mind) that you're simplifying something for your short-term purposes, knowing perfectly well that "it's not exactly like that."

Here's my simplification: the left brain is analytical, linear, oriented toward data that it (the left brain) has tools to measure. The right brain is intuitive, sensorial, nonlinear, free from the benefits and constraints of measuring. The liminal experience places you in between the left and right brain, using both at the same time in a confused and confusing dialogue.

An astute student of mine once said, "Lack of clarity sometimes *is* the clarity." When you're in the liminal territory, you may find that things, ideas, situations, and people lack clarity. And yet things, ideas, situations, and people then become true to their own selves, their own kaleidoscopic, shifting, multidimensional selves (Figure 16.7).

Figure 16.7 Knowledge and mystery at work. Credit: Vinit Kumar.

CONCLUSION

This is a strange book—I'm the first to admit it. An octopus dancing a slow flamenco under water; Old Joe, a piano so enfeebled as to be unplayable, and yet the author of the book tells you that you should love Old Joe, even venerate it; Richard Nixon arriving in Brazil and greeting the populace with the OK sign, oh what a scandal; sponges and kitchen towels, which you squeeze and caress in lieu of practicing scales and arpeggios; counting a hundred beans, one by one, slowly, carefully, in ecstasy. And all of this is supposed to help your hands, wrists, and fingers.

I'm teasing myself for having thought up the strange book and for offering it to you, the unsuspecting reader. Truth be told, I stand by the book. I think I'm onto something. I'm convinced that the octopus will help your hands, wrists, and fingers (Figure C.1).

It's an inescapable fact that a human being—every human being—is made of irreconcilable urges, inconsistent emotions, incoherent opinions, unwarranted assumptions and suppositions, blind spots. And it's also an inescapable fact that a human being—every human being—has incredible inner resources and potentialities, including imagination, resilience, and adaptability. We're all made of hope and fear, reason and unreason, goodness and not-so-goodness. We are complex and complicated. We try to cope with the complicated play of opposing forces raging inside us by separating the forces and handling them in isolation. Intellect and intuition, separated; left brain and right brain, separated; art and science, separated; nature and science, separated; fact and fiction, separated; consciousness and the unconscious, separated. Separation is meant to help us understand things and control them. And separation has indeed helped some people deal with some of their concerns some of the time. Separation has its merits, and it's entitled to claim many victories.

Separation, however, also carries risks and dangers. The human being is a totality. We can't separate our behaviors from our family histories; we can't separate our pains from our fears; we can't separate our fears from our assumptions and suppositions; we can't separate our musical techniques from our aesthetics; we can't separate our aesthetics from our grasp of the

Figure C.1 Marvel. Credit: Swastik Arora.

Figure C.2 Unified purpose. Credit: sarab123.

Figure C.3 The growth of unified purpose. Credit: Ben Kerckx.

musical language, its grammar, its orthography and punctuation, its formal structures, its prosody; we can't separate our hands, wrists, and fingers from our imaginations, our family histories, our fears, our assumptions and suppositions, our techniques and aesthetics, our ability to speak the language of music. Separation itself is a contributing cause of many awkward hands, wrists, and fingers; sometimes, separation itself is the ultimate cause of the handicaps and concerns challenging our use of our hands, wrists, and fingers (Figures C.2 and C.3).

The totality is an iceberg; the hands, wrists, and fingers are the tip of the iceberg. Rightly or wrongly, in this book I've attempted to address the totality rather than the tip. Let me say it differently: I've attempted to address the tip by referring ceaselessly to the totality, using storytelling, jokes, paradoxes, arguments, photos, and video clips. And exercises; I did offer you some exercises, didn't I?

Figure C.4 The results of imagination. Credit: Christopher Chilton.

What is the single most important dimension of the human totality? It's the human imagination. Johann Sebastian Bach had to imagine the St. Matthew Passion. Niccolò Paganini had to imagine revolutionary techniques that no one else had imagined before him. Franz Liszt had to imagine the Romantic concert artist as an adored star. You've had to imagine yourself as a musician, whether you're a professional or an amateur, whether music is the whole of your life or a small part of it. Imagination has created musical instruments, concert halls, competitions, compositions, improvisations, pedagogies. Imagination had to create Shinichi Suzuki, so that Suzuki could create Suzuki. Imagination has created problems, and imagination has found solutions.

Dancing a slow flamenco under water, my beloved octopus exists in my imagination only. Nevertheless, imagining its absurd flamenco has an energizing effect on me. I behave differently when the octopus is in my mind's foreground. I feel more flexible, more fluid, more adaptable; I connect with my own animal nature; I start moving my arms, hands, wrists, and fingers in a peculiar way, because in my imagination I've become the octopus. If you prefer, I'll rephrase it and say that I've become just a little bit more octopus-like in some of my motions (Figure C.4).

Imagining the octopus helps me. Imagining that each musical instrument has a soul helps me. It helps me to imagine that the Goddess of Nothing

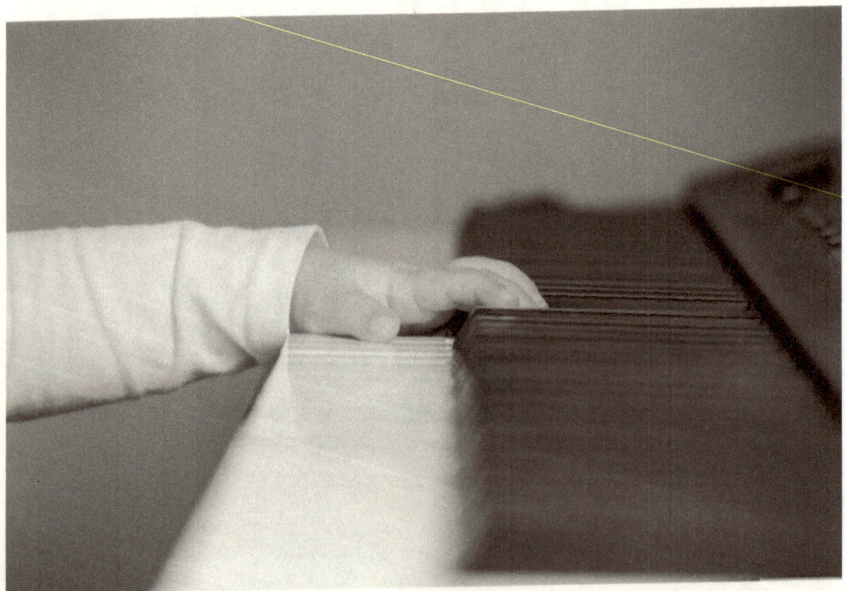

Figure C.5 Infinite potentiality. Credit: Rosalia Ricotta.

plays the cello for me, as long as I stay out of her way. Buckminster Fuller and Kenneth Snelson imagined tensegrity as a practical force in architecture and engineering. Using my imagination, I captured their discovery and transposed it to my inner reality: I imagined myself as a living and breathing tensegrity structure. I'm aware that the transposition is idiosyncratic, poetic, inexact; let's say that the original tensegrity is material and objective to some extent, and my tensegrity is subjective and dematerialized to some extent. Theirs and mine are two different animals, dwelling in two different forests. But it helps me to transpose their concept, to steal it, to own it as my deeply embodied reality. Thanks to my stealing, I play better, I sound better, I move better, I live better.

This is Creative Health at work (Figure C.5).

APPENDIX I

Illustrative Video Clips

I put together a collection of informal videos inspired by the themes from *Hands, Wrists, Fingers*. These aren't instructional videos that explain the book's exercises, but performances in which I respond to ideas from the book. I didn't aim to be comprehensive. Instead, I selected a few concepts and recorded my confrontations with them—partly for my pleasure, and partly to invite you to play the game in turn. Many clips feature my own compositions and improvisations. Below I list all the compositions I used, including those by other composers. I didn't think it was necessary to title or credit my improvisations. "Scordatura" refers to unorthodox tunings for string instruments.

The video clips are posted on the book's dedicated online page, hosted by Anthem Press. Look for the Links menu here: https://anthempress.com/hands-wrists-fingers-pb.

Chapter 2, "The Body is Culture"

1. Painted Hands ("Boy Joy," for solo cello in scordatura, and "Parade," for Native American flute)

Chapter 5, "Expressive Gesticulation"

2. Expressive Gesticulation
3. Speedy Gesticulation ("Puro Açúcar," for voice and cello in scordatura)
4. From the Elbow
5. Coincidence ("Convocation," for solo cello in scordatura)

Chapter 6, "Sounds Made and Sounds Heard"

6. Clapping

Chapter 7, "The Dance"

7. Walking Fingers
8. Dance of the Wrists ("Shadows," for solo cello in scordatura)
9. Dance of the Fists ("Sunshine," for voice and piano)

Chapter 8, "Textures"

10. Skin, Flesh, Bones 1 ("Bassist," for solo cello in scordatura)
11. Skin, Flesh, Bones 2 ("In the Japanese Garden," for solo cello)

Chapter 9, "Object Wisdom: A Manifesto"

12. All Instruments: French Horn
13. All Instruments: Cymbals
14. All Instruments: Piano ("Venus Rising," for solo piano)
15. All Instruments: Cello ("Shadow Boxing," for solo cello)
16. All Instruments: Native American Flute ("Tremolo," for flute and voice)

Chapter 10, "Object Wisdom: A Workshop"

17. Juggling Balls ("Low Tide, Dawn," for solo cello in scordatura)
18. The Thread
19. Object Wisdom: The Bow ("Hypnosis," for solo cello in scordatura)
20. Object Wisdom: The Flute ("To Dust Again," for Native American flute and voice, on an excerpt from Ecclesiastes)

Chapter 11, "Strength Redefined"

21. Destroy a Newspaper
22. Knead a Pillow ("Modinha" by Francisco Mignone, for cello and piano; with Fabio Gardenal, piano)

Chapter 12, "Repetitive Practice"

23. Rotations and Percussions ("Maranhão," for solo guitar in scordatura)
24. Articulations ("Hexagram," for solo guitar in scordatura)
25. Index Finger ("Frets," for solo guitar in scordatura)
26. Thumb Strum
27. Interpretative Repetition ("I Have Something to Say," for voice and cello in scordatura)

28. Infinite Repetition
29. Drawing ("After Bartók," for solo cello in scordatura)
30. Erasing ("Alma Brasileira" by Heitor Villa-Lobos, arranged for cello and piano by Pedro de Alcantara; with Fabio Gardenal, piano)
31. Counting Beans ("El Mariachi," for solo cello in scordatura)

Chapter 13, "Energy"

32. Energy ("The Yemenite," for solo cello in scordatura)
33. The Pleasures of Ice ("Ponticello," for solo cello)

Chapter 14, "Animality and Healing"

34. Animality ("Climb, Climb, Climb," for voice and piano)
35. Cat's Ballet ("Tico-Tico," for voice and Native American flute, inspired by the song "Tico-Tico no Fubá" by Zequinha de Abreu)
36. Enveloping (Sonata for cello and piano, opus 6: second movement, by Samuel Barber; with Fabio Gardenal, piano)

APPENDIX II

Suggested Reading

The ideal library is infinite, and the ideal librarian knows exactly what you're looking for. My suggested reading list is the antithesis of that ideal: it's laughably incomplete, and I really don't know what you're looking for. And yet, you might luck out and find something useful when my subjectivity briefly meets yours.

I wrote multiple books for musicians that address creative health directly or indirectly. Here they are, in order of publication.

- *Indirect Procedures: A Musician's Guide to the Alexander Technique* (Oxford University Press, 1997; fully rewritten second edition, 2013). The first edition has been translated into French (2000), German (2002), and Japanese (2009). The second edition has been translated into Chinese, simplified characters (2018). The Alexander Technique lends itself to many interpretations and applications. Mine might be abbreviated like this: Become alert to the connections that organize and determine your existence: connections among body parts; connections among the physical, the mental, and the aesthetic dimensions; connections from gesture to gesture, from thought to gesture, from thought to thought, from thought to speech; connections between you and music itself, connections between you and the audience.
- *The Alexander Technique: A Skill for Life* (Crowood Press, 1999; fully rewritten second edition, 2021). The first edition has been translated into Japanese (2010) and Estonian (2013). This is a much shorter book, not specifically for musicians.
- *Integrated Practice: Coordination, Rhythm & Practice* (Oxford University Press, 2011). Here I attempt to show you how to develop rhythmic and linguistic clarity. To play music is to speak the language of music. The clearer you are about what you're saying musically, the freer you become as a musician. A dedicated page on the publisher's website holds 72 video clips and 25 audio clips covering the book's materials.

- *The Integrated String Player: Embodied Vibration* (Oxford University Press, 2018). For players of bowed instruments (violin, viola, cello, double bass, viola da gamba, etc.). A dedicated page on the publisher's website holds 80 video clips and 10 audio clips covering the book's materials.
- *Creative Health for Pianists: Concepts, Exercises, Compositions* (Oxford University Press, 2023). Here I present the piano as a tool for exploration, discovery, and—for accomplished pianists—rediscovery. A dedicated page on the publisher's website holds 48 video clips illustrating the book's materials.

Although the subject of hands is vast, relatively few books have covered the subject in detail or in depth. Among the existing books, some take a scholarly or academic approach that I find difficult to follow. This may reflect my own limitations, rather than the writers'. Here is a handful of readable books.

- *Hands,* John Napier (Princeton University Press, 1980; new edition, revised by Russell H. Tuttle, 1993). An interesting book covering grounds similar to mine, but with greater brevity and elegance.
- *Hands: What We Do with Them—and Why,* Darian Leader (Penguin, 2017). Cultural reflections and anecdotes on the role of hands.
- *The Human Hand,* Charlotte Wolff (Routledge, originally published in 1942). An astute psychologist explores temperament and behavior by studying the construction of hands. May I offer you a teasing opinion that, for me, encapsulates a small part of her work? "Palm readers are frauds. But, wait! They are on to something!" Her book isn't about palmistry; my remark hints at the liminality of her explorations.

And since we're here, let me mention Cheiro (born William John Warner): occultist, astrologer, palm reader, and wonderfully compelling writer. His book *Cheiro's Language of the Hand* (1894) is available as a free pdf on the Internet. Very entertaining! You don't need to believe in palmistry to enjoy Cheiro's company and to think differently about hands.

An early reader of my manuscript was reminded of two other books, both about mindfulness. "Mindfulness isn't a book, but a walk in the park," I once overheard someone say. Nevertheless, here are the books in question.

- *Zen in the Art of Archery,* Eugen Herrigel. First published in 1948 and now available in multiple editions from different editors. The book has received its share of harsh criticism, but the main thing about any book is not what the book says but what you make of it.
- *The Inner Game of Tennis,* W. Timothy Gallwey (Random House, 1974).

INDEX

abaissement du niveau mental 93–94
accoutrements 31–34
actor, receptor, witness 168–70
aikido 17
Alexander Technique 17
allowed and forbidden 27–29
animality: appetites 205
   and enveloping 212–16
   and gut feeling 207
   and the inner animal 4, 7, 205–9
   leap of the imagination 216–19
   and muscular effort 201
   playfulness 207
   stuffed toys 209–12
animism 122, 211
appearing and disappearing 197–201
archetype: 33–35
   Brush 224
   Cat 103
   Cup 221
   First-Time 47, 50–52
   Fist 216
   Flute 126–28
   Gesture 226
   Henna 35–38
   Keyboard 125–29
   Mask 34–35
   musical instruments 125–29
   Paper 130
   Ring 33–34
   Ritual 230
asymmetry 57–59

Bach, Johann Sebastian 50, 97, 221–24, 236, 246
Bauhaus 140
Beethoven, Ludwig van 1–3, 172
blues 172
bones 45
Bonomi, Carlo 81
Buddha 77, 140

Cage, John 173
clapping 87–90
coincidence (exercise) 84–85
commedia dell'arte 81–82
containment 85
counting beans 175–80
Creative Health: and choices 3
   and coherence 4
   defined 1–3
   and emotions 4
   and first-person singular 4
   healing 5–7
   learning processes 90
   and literal-mindedness 209
   paradoxes 141
   and responding to a music score 5
   and a temporary decline in judgment 95
culture and the body: accoutrements 31–34
   acupuncture 22
   allowed and forbidden 27–29
   anatomy 22
   chakras 25
   henna 35–38
   masks 34–35
   mysticism 25–26
   self–identification 28–29
   touch 29–31
   Ze 25–26

dance: of hands and fingers 97–100
   of wrists 100–101
database: of energies 190
   of exercises 5
   of gestures 71, 85
   and latencies 4
demiurge 2
destroying a newspaper 157–61
discovery: and changeability 43–44
   and looking and lingering 40–42

and memory 50–52
and observing 42
and vocabulary 44–47
and wonderment 39
drawing 172–75

embodied narrative 62
energy: appearing and disappearing 197–201
  in conducting 185
  and effort 200–202
  of hands 187
  of handshakes 185
  heat and cold 190–92
  latency 202–4
  light and heavy 192–94
  list of potentialities 203
  make-believe and playacting 185–87
  and pointing 187–90
  propagation and containment 194–97

First–Time 47, 50–52
fist 72, 80, 197, 213–16
flamenco 14, 90, 98, 103–4, 243, 246
Fuller, R. Buckminster 149, 247

gesticulation: and coincidence (exercise) 84–85
  gestural choreography 80
  and grammelot 80–83
  linguistic organization 14–15
  mudra 77–79
  the OK sign 77
  and personal styles 75
  and the power of a single gesture 75, 77
  using a pencil 83–84
Gismonti, Egberto 228
Goddess of Nothing 200, 246–47
Gould, Glenn 11
gradations 167–68
grammelot 80–83
Gropius, Walter 140

Hardy, Thomas 101
henna 35–38

imagination 101–4, 115, 200, 216–20, 238, 246–47
improvisation: seemingly aimless 100
  and clapping 90
  and *commedia dell'arte* 81
  fear of 2
  and gesticulation 139

Gismonti 228
improvisational theater 94
and intentionality 77–81
as liminality 232
and Mozart 5, 216
and structure 18
inner animal 4, 7, 205–9
intellectual placebo 186–87

Janet, Pierre 93
juggling balls 135–39
Jung, Carl 93–94

knuckles 45–46

latency: and containment 85
  and health 4
  latent energies 202–4
  and the latent generalist within 133
  latent resistance and mobility 166
  and totality 55
left-handedness 58–59
liminality: believing and unbelieving 235–36
  and concert attire 235
  dancing with the absurd 236–39
  defined 231–32
  Elvis Presley 232
  and entering the stage 232–33
  metronome and rubato 235
  and palm reading 238–39
  and the passage between private and public 233–35
Liszt, Franz 246

make-believe and playacting 185–87
masks 34–35
megaphone 90, 92–93
mething 58
Mozart, Wolfgang Amadeus 5, 98
mudra 77–79

nails: characteristics 46–49
  and associated rituals 230
  claw-like 47–49
  loss and regrowth 60
  and self-consciousness 57
  and social pressure 28
Nimoy, Leonard 13
Nixon, Richard 77, 243

Object Wisdom: and animism 122
  and book pages 140–43

and developing discernment 122
as dialogue with objects 122, 124
instruments as archetypes 125–29
integration 145–47
and juggling balls 135–39
and literal-mindedness 124
and musical aesthetics 131
paradoxes 141
and a stick of wood 144–45
and a thread 143–44
and a toothbrush 119
octopus 103–4, 243
Old Joe 129–31, 243
Onetti, Juan Carlos 101–2

Paganini, Niccolò 246
palm reading 238–39
paradigm: defined 11, 18–19
 left–brain 11–12
 right–brain 12–13
 risks and dangers 16–18
Pingu 80–81
Presley, Elvis 232
propagation and containment 194–97

raspberry 94
repetitive practice: and actor, receptor, witness 168–70
 counting beans 175–80
 drawing 172–75
 and gradations 167–68
 and the linguistic impulse 170–72
 and making choices 165–66
 and musical materials 180–82
 and organizing yourself 166–67
rings 33–34
risks and dangers 16–18
ritual: accoutrements 23–24
 of daily life 221–22
 defined 228
 and dialogue with objects 226
 of fixtures 224–25
 of hand care 229–30
 paradox of integration 222
 of personal hygiene 222–24

ritualistic possibilities 158
and rosin 227
on stage 228
and wisdom of children 228
rosin 227
rubber bands 153–57
Rubinstein, Artur 11

Schubert, Franz 172
separation and totality 243–44
shaolin salute 213–16
sight-reading 5
simplification 11, 59, 62, 240
Snelson, Kenneth 149, 247
stick of wood 144–45
story: of accidents and hurts 59–62
 embodied narratives 62
 and introducing the hands 56–57
 mething 58
 sensuality 65–66
 and skills and crafts 62–65
strength: destroying a newspaper 157–61
 distributed resistance 151–53
 kneading 161–63
 rubber bands 153–57
 tensegrity 149–50
Suzuki, Shinichi 246

taboo 29, 31, 58–59, 75–77, 159, 187
teddy bear 209–12
tensegrity 149–50, 157, 247
texture: of cello strings 109, 111
 of diverse objects 115–18
 in making dinner 107
 of paper 111–14
 of textiles 108–9
 and walking barefoot 107
thread 143–44
Tolstoy, Leo 5
touch 29–31

vocabulary 44–47, 53, 55–56

Wagner, Richard 33
washing hands 53–54

www.ingramcontent.com/pod-product-compliance
Lightning Source LLC
Chambersburg PA
CBHW022011300426
44117CB00005B/123